RAND NATIONAL DEFENSE RESEARCH INSTITUTE

T0294855

Are Current Military Education Benefits Efficient and Effective for the Services?

Jennie W. Wenger, Trey Miller, Matthew D. Baird, Peter Buryk, Lindsay Daugherty, Marlon Graf, Simon Hollands, Salar Jahedi, Douglas Yeung

Prepared for the Office of the Secretary of Defense

Approved for public release; distribution unlimited

For more information on this publication, visit www.rand.org/t/RR1766

Library of Congress Cataloging-in-Publication Data is available for this publication.
ISBN: 978-0-8330-9806-1

Published by the RAND Corporation, Santa Monica, Calif.
© Copyright 2017 RAND Corporation
RAND® is a registered trademark.

Cover image by carlofranco, Getty Images.

Limited Print and Electronic Distribution Rights

This document and trademark(s) contained herein are protected by law. This representation of RAND intellectual property is provided for noncommercial use only. Unauthorized posting of this publication online is prohibited. Permission is given to duplicate this document for personal use only, as long as it is unaltered and complete. Permission is required from RAND to reproduce, or reuse in another form, any of its research documents for commercial use. For information on reprint and linking permissions, please visit www.rand.org/pubs/permissions.

The RAND Corporation is a research organization that develops solutions to public policy challenges to help make communities throughout the world safer and more secure, healthier and more prosperous. RAND is nonprofit, nonpartisan, and committed to the public interest.

RAND's publications do not necessarily reflect the opinions of its research clients and sponsors.

Support RAND
Make a tax-deductible charitable contribution at
www.rand.org/giving/contribute

www.rand.org

Preface

Since the end of World War II, U.S. service members have had access to benefits to support the pursuit of higher education. A primary focus of these benefits has been assisting the service member's transition back to civilian life. In the current era, service members have access to a variety of education benefits for use while in the military and after. In particular, service members have access to the Post-9/11 GI Bill, a generous benefit passed in 2008 that includes funds for tuition and other expenses, as well as a living allowance. While in the military, service members have access to Tuition Assistance. Research suggests these benefits improve service members' long-term outcomes (such as labor force participation, earnings, and job satisfaction). However, these substantial benefits might also be expected to influence shorter-term outcomes, such as recruiting and retention.

At this point, sufficient time has passed to make it possible to assess key aspects of the Post-9/11 GI Bill. Therefore, the Office of the Under Secretary of Defense for Personnel and Readiness requested that RAND examine the two largest education benefits, the Post-9/11 GI Bill and Tuition Assistance, with a focus on impacts on recruiting and retention and the potential for interactions between these benefits. This research should be of interest to policymakers concerned with education benefits, as well as to those interested in how benefits influence recruiting, retention, and other outcomes, and those interested in compensation for service members more broadly.

This research was sponsored by the Under Secretary of Defense for Personnel and Readiness and conducted within the Forces and Resources Policy Center of RAND's National Defense Research Institute, a federally funded research and development center sponsored by the Office of the Secretary of Defense, the Joint Staff, the Unified Combatant Commands, the Department of the Navy, the Marine Corps, the defense agencies, and the defense Intelligence Community. For more information on the RAND Forces and Resources Policy Center, see www.rand.org/nsrd/ndri/centers/frp or contact the director (contact information is provided on the web page).

Contents

Figures

Tables

Summary

The Department of Defense (DoD) is committed to investing in the education of service members and veterans. Today's higher education assistance programs, like the original GI Bill in 1944, are designed to support service members' transitions to civilian life. There is evidence that some programs have achieved this goal, with studies suggesting that military members who receive higher education benefits and complete their courses of study enjoy high earnings in the civilian world (see, e.g., Loughran et al., 2011).

What is uncertain, however, is how these programs affect DoD. Educational assistance programs have the potential to attract people into service and thus have a positive effect on recruiting. But these benefits may also shorten the service time of some members, as higher education improves their career prospects in the civilian world. Moreover, it is unknown how the different higher educational assistance programs complement one another in relation to recruiting, retention, and educational outcomes.

To gain a fuller understanding of the effects of today's DoD education assistance programs on the military workforce, the Under Secretary of Defense for Personnel and Readiness (USD[P&R]) asked the RAND Corporation to address the following questions:

- How do military education benefits influence recruiting?
- How do military education benefits influence retention?

Our sponsor also expressed interest in the ways that different education benefit programs could work together, and recommendations that could make existing benefits more efficient or effective.

Study Scope and Methods

The team focused on the two most substantial DoD education assistance programs, the Post-9/11 GI Bill (PGIB) and Tuition Assistance (TA). These two programs make up the bulk of DoD spending in this area. The PGIB was introduced and passed in

2008. This benefit recaptures the spirit of the original GI Bill by paying tuition at a wide variety of institutions, and by including a living allowance as well as funds for books and other expenses. While the PGIB can be used by veterans and current service members, its structure is more suited toward veterans intending to enroll in college full time, and indeed the vast majority of PGIB users have been separated veterans. The PGIB also includes a more unusual feature—those who qualify for the bill may divide its 36 months of benefits between themselves and one or more dependent(s). The PGIB has been utilized by well over 1 million (current and former) service members and by over 200,000 dependents.

TA provides funds for tuition (within certain limits) for service members who wish to pursue higher education while serving. This benefit, too, is widely used; service members took over 9 million courses with TA funds between 2003 and 2015. There are small variations in this program across the services, but all versions pay for the cost of tuition with per–credit hour and per-year limits.

Obtaining higher education through TA or the PGIB would be expected to have a substantial impact on eventual civilian earnings; accruing degrees or credits through these programs might also influence job placement, occupation, job satisfaction, and other long-term outcomes of former service members.

As a generous benefit available to the vast majority of service members in the era following the terrorist attacks of September 11, 2001, the PGIB might also be expected to have an impact both on recruiting and on retention. Transferring the benefit to dependents requires an additional service commitment, so this aspect of the benefit, too, could be expected to have an impact on retention. TA might also be expected to affect shorter-term outcomes during service. Finally, it appears quite possible that TA and the PGIB might work together; service members may strategically use the two benefits to maximize desired educational outcomes.

Due to the wide variety of potential effects of these benefits, we utilized a "lifetime" approach rather than focusing on only one or a few points in a service member's career. Figure S.1 depicts the concept of education benefit evolution and use during a typical service career trajectory.

The green, purple, and orange boxes in the figure depict the various data sources and approaches used to collect service members' knowledge and use of education benefits. The team collected enlistment, education, and service data from multiple sources, including the Defense Manpower Data Center, the U.S. Department of Veterans Affairs (VA) (the Defense Manpower Data Center also provided VA data), individual service branches, Status of Forces surveys, and Internet search results. The team also conduced interviews with eight college counselors specializing in military students at colleges and held numerous focus groups with new service members. Both qualitative and quantitative approaches were used in assessing the collected data.

Figure S.1
Conceptual Framework for Education Benefits Decisionmaking Process

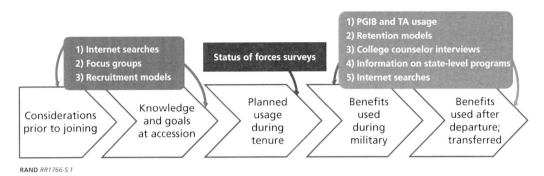

RAND *RR1766-S.1*

Findings

Post-9/11 GI Bill Benefits Appear to Play a Small Positive Role in Attracting Potential Recruits

The Post-9/11 GI Bill does appear to attract additional high-quality recruits. Our analyses of administrative data generally indicate that the proportion of high-quality recruits increased slightly after the PGIB was passed. Some of this increase does not seem to be linked to other factors (such as the civilian economy). We find generally similar results when we examine the proportion of recruits with Armed Forces Qualification Test (AFQT) scores in the top quartile. This indicates that the passage of the PGIB had a small positive effect on the quality of recruits.

Many New Recruits Know That Education Benefits Exist but Lack Insight on Details

Results from new-recruit focus groups suggest that a general awareness of benefits, rather than specific restrictions or benefit components, is likely to be driving enlistment decisions. Focus groups participants were generally aware of education benefits but lacked detailed knowledge. Some recruits did appear better informed than others. Recruits informed about details were generally older, more likely to have prior experience with college, more likely to be female, and less likely to be entering the Marines. But as a group, new recruits lacked insight that would allow them to appreciate the substantial increase in benefit generosity that the PGIB represents. While we designed our focus groups to include a variety of new recruits, the groups included small numbers, and the results may not be generally representative of all new recruits.

Consistent with this finding, our analyses of Internet search data indicate that questions about educational opportunities in the services are unlikely to form the basis of most initial explorations into military enlistment. Instead, searches more often focus on aspects of life in the service, the procedures and requirements for joining, and pay. As we discuss below, while service members appear to learn more about education benefits throughout their time in the military, we find some evidence that experienced service members still lack detailed information.

Intention to Use Education Benefits Has Increased over Time

Multiple waves of data collected over a decade through the Status of Forces surveys suggest that intentions to use education benefits change throughout a service member's military career. Over time, those completing the survey have become more likely to indicate that money for college played a role in their decision to join the military. Especially among those without dependents, service members are also likely to state that continuing their education is a reason they consider leaving the military. The data also demonstrated a modest increase in the level of spousal education, which suggests that spouses may be increasingly interested in education benefits. There was also a small decrease over time in the proportion who reported earning college credit while in the military.

Passage of the PGIB Has a Small Negative Effect on Continuation, Which the Transfer Option Appears to Mitigate Somewhat

Our results indicate that continuation did decrease after the passage of the PGIB, and that some of the decrease cannot be explained by other factors. Passage of the PGIB appears to be associated with a 2– to 3–percentage point drop in continuation. This finding is consistent with some service members exiting the military to use the PGIB. We also find that the decrease in continuation was smaller among those with dependents than among service members without dependents; in other words, the transfer option appears to have mitigated some of the negative effects on continuation. This is consistent with the intent of the transfer aspect of the PGIB.

Our Limited Interviews with College Advisors Suggest That Some Enrolled Service Members and Veterans May Lack Understanding of PGIB Benefits

We spoke to a limited number of college advisors. Information gathered in these interviews indicates that even after enrolling, some military and veteran students still lack detailed knowledge about their education benefits. In particular, they lack understanding of the underlying procedures and requirements related to the PGIB. Advisors related this to the complex nature of the PGIB benefits and a perceived lack of guidance from military sources. Additionally, advisors also indicated concern that many of these students do not think strategically about how to utilize their various benefits and combine them effectively with other sources of support. However, current service members using the TA program were perceived to be generally well informed about their TA benefits.

TA and PGIB Benefits Complement Each Other Rather Than Overlap

Finally, the data suggest that TA and the PGIB work in concert. Even after the 2008 passage of PGIB, service members have continued to use TA. Indeed, passage of the PGIB is associated with a small increase in TA usage. In this context, TA could represent an opportunity for those service members who choose to attend a four-year college on the PGIB to increase the probability of completing a degree within the confines of their PGIB benefits. We also find that those who use TA and/or PGIB are more likely than others to be promoted, even though PGIB usage occurs after the promotion decision. However, we note that TA and PGIB operate separately from each other. Coordination between the two programs could prove beneficial.

Recommendations

The findings from this study can be divided into two main groups: those that concern knowledge and use of education benefits, and those that concern force management issues. Additionally, we provide some suggestions for future research to further improve understanding of how service members learn about and use education benefits. We take up each group of recommendations in turn.

Knowledge and Use of Education Benefits

In general, our results indicate that new service members lack a detailed understanding of education benefits. While service members appear to gain substantial understanding over time, the limited number of interviews we undertook with college advisors suggests that even at the point of school enrollment (generally after leaving the military), some service members may still lack key information. Therefore, *we recommend providing additional information to service members at key points in time.*

Specific examples include *providing additional or more targeted information to potential recruits.* This could increase potential recruits' knowledge—and appreciation—of education benefits. Also, *expanding and/or making mandatory counseling services for first-time PGIB users* could assist students in finding the most effective pathways to reach their educational goals (thereby increasing the effectiveness of education benefits in terms of degree or credential attainment). *Expanding and continuing to fine-tune the GI Bill Comparison Tool* could pay dividends as well. The VA has partnered with the U.S. Department of Education and DoD to develop this online tool that provides information that can help service members and dependent beneficiaries search for appropriate colleges to utilize their benefits (VA, undated). The tool includes useful information about completion rates of different credentials and earnings of graduates at eligible institutions. Such information can be helpful in choosing appropriate programs that can allow service members to complete useful credentials in a timely manner and potentially lowering costs. Finally, *providing key information about benefit and transfer options and requirements to those who are nearing the end of an enlistment term or who are nearing transfer eligibility* could increase effectiveness.

We note specifically that we do not know exactly how much information is provided to service members in the current system; it is possible that key information is already provided to service members and that some simply do not retain the information. Determining what is provided/retained currently would be a key first step in expanding service members' knowledge of benefits.

Our analyses indicate that the TA program delivers educational credits at a lower cost than PGIB. Also, obtaining credit through TA could place service members in a better position to determine the appropriate course of study under the PGIB and could place them in a better position to complete a degree within the time frame allowed by the PGIB. Therefore, *encouraging the use of the TA program* has the potential to decrease costs and possibly increase degree completion.

Force Management and Force Shaping

Our analyses find that that the recent increase in education benefits represented by passage of the PGIB has had only a small influence on attracting potential recruits. The passage of the benefit is also linked to a decrease in continuation rates, but the decrease is smaller among those who have dependents. This suggests that the provision to transfer the PGIB to dependents has, as intended, encouraged some service members to remain in the military. But the impact on continuation rates has been relatively modest as well. Based on these results, we recommend that DoD *continue to focus on traditional tools, such as bonuses, to achieve force management.* Indeed, while DoD should do as much as possible to ensure that education programs serve to benefit the Department and assist service members in obtaining their goals, our results suggest that changes to education benefits are unlikely to have large, substantial impacts on key aspects of force management (namely, recruiting and retention). Fortunately, other tools have been shown to be effective in addressing force management objectives.

Of course, *continued careful tracking of recruit quality and retention metrics* should remain an area of focus. Such tracking would likely become especially important if, for example, there were sudden changes to the cost of college or changes to the benefits provided through the PGIB or TA.

Finally, given the evidence of interaction between TA and PGIB, we recommend *carefully calibrating the alignment between DoD and VA on changes to the PGIB.* Carefully coordinating any changes to the PGIB could assist DoD and the services in obtaining their goals related to recruitment and retention. At present, it is not clear that specific mechanisms for such coordination are in place.

Additional Research to Further Improve Understanding of Education Benefits

We recommend that DoD invest in multimethod approaches to better understand service members' experiences with education benefits, and the extent to which they are achieving their primary objectives. The data collected for this study did not enable the team to determine which service members and dependents complete degrees or programs. This information would be extremely helpful in making more overarching determinations of the effectiveness of these programs.

Also, we recommend that future research focus on *forecasting the costs of education benefits* moving forward. An important consideration for future policy decisions around military education benefits should be the overall costs of providing those benefits. By all measures, these are high. The current annual cost of the PGIB alone is more than $10 billion. However, it is beyond the scope of the current project to estimate the total costs of these benefits over time.

Acknowledgments

First, we thank the Office of the Undersecretary of Defense for Personnel and Readiness. Specifically, we thank our project monitors, Dennis Drogo and Evelyn Dyer, who worked closely with us throughout our research and who provided a great deal of assistance to us as we worked to coordinate the focus groups with new recruits. We also thank Stephanie Miller and Christopher Arendt, who provided helpful guidance as we conducted our research. Jerilyn Busch, Patricia Leopard, and Robert Clark also provided helpful comments and guidance through the research process. Dawn Bilodeau and Jonathan Woods of Department of Defense Voluntary Education provided invaluable assistance as we worked to obtain data on Tuition Assistance. Vince Suich of the Defense Manpower Data Center (DMDC) provided assistance with the Post-9/11 GI Bill data; Michael DiNicolantonio of DMDC provided assistance with the Status of Forces data; Scott Seggerman of DMDC repeatedly provided assistance throughout the project with several different data sets.

Catherine Augustine of RAND and Michael Kofoed of the U.S. Military Academy provided reviews that ensured our work met RAND's high standards for quality. We also benefited from the contributions of other RAND colleagues; in particular, Jim Hosek and Beth Asch provided guidance and insights that were very helpful to us, while Craig Bond reviewed several versions of the document. Barbara Bicksler and Paul Steinberg assisted us in preparing briefings. Cynthia Christopher and Katherine Mariska provided administrative support. John Winkler also provided guidance throughout the course of this project.

Finally, we note that we could not have completed this work without the insights provided by new recruits as well as those provided in confidential focus groups and discussions by personnel at military and veterans' student offices at a small number of postsecondary institutions.

We thank all who contributed to this research, but of course we retain full responsibility for the objectivity, accuracy, and analytic integrity of the work presented here.

Abbreviations

ADPF	Active Duty Pay File
AFQT	Armed Forces Qualifying Test
ASVAB	Armed Services Vocational Aptitude Battery
BAH	basic allowance for housing
DEERS	Defense Enrollment Eligibility Reporting System
DEP	Delayed Entry Program
DMDC	Defense Manpower Data Center
DoD	U.S. Department of Defense
HRSAP	Human Resources Strategic Assessment Program
IVG	Illinois Veteran Grant
MEPCOM	U.S. Military Entrance and Processing Command
MGIB	Montgomery GI Bill
MtF	Monitoring the Future
PGIB	Post 9/11 GI Bill
RPF	Reserve Pay File
SOF	Status of Forces (Survey of Active Duty Members)
TA	Tuition Assistance
USD(P&R)	Under Secretary of Defense for Personnel and Readiness

VA	U.S. Department of Veterans Affairs
WEX	Work Experience File
WGIB	Wisconsin GI Bill
YATS	Youth Attitude Tracking Study

CHAPTER ONE

Introduction

The U.S. Department of Defense (DoD) has long been committed to investing in the education of service members and veterans. Today's education assistance programs, such as the Post-9/11 GI Bill (PGIB, or "Chapter 33") and Tuition Assistance (TA), are designed in part to support service member transition to civilian life in ways that are similar to the original Servicemen's Readjustment Act of 1944 or "GI Bill" (Pub. L. 78-346, 1944); that is, they compensate service members for the sacrifices made during service by making provisions for their economic well-being during the transition to the civilian world (U.S. Department of Veterans Affairs, 2013). Indeed, several studies in the past decade have demonstrated that many service members and veterans benefit from these programs: Briefly, the relationship between military service, education benefits, and education attainment is a positive one that can result in increased civilian earnings for former service members (see Loughran et al., 2011).

While the commitment to service member and veteran quality-of-life is an enduring factor of DoD education assistance programs, less is known how about such programs affect DoD. More specifically, support for higher education is a benefit and, as such, it has a potential effect on the DoD workforce. Postsecondary education is costly, and a tuition benefit may influence people's decision to enlist in the military. In turn, as education is gained, a service member's economic prospects may improve in the civilian world, which might ultimately motivate him or her to leave service; finally, the compensation to attend college may influence some service members' retention decisions. Some insight into how programs affect military enlistment and retention has been gleaned through studies focused on earlier programs such as the 1984 Montgomery GI Bill (MGIB). To date, however, there is very limited information on how new DoD education benefits are affecting enlistment and retention, and there is no examination of how different educational assistance programs complement or substitute for one another in relation to recruiting, retention, and educational outcomes.

To gain a fuller understanding of the effects of today's DoD education assistance programs on the military workforce, the Under Secretary of Defense for Personnel and Readiness (USD[P&R]) asked the RAND Corporation to address the following questions:

- How do military education benefits influence recruiting?
- How do military education benefits influence retention?
- To what extent do military personnel use military education programs separately or together to further their education?

The study elicited findings and recommendations for USD(P&R) leadership to consider as they work to improve the efficacy and efficiency of military education assistance programs.

Research Scope: Post-9/11 GI Bill and Tuition Assistance

This study focuses on two substantial DoD education assistance programs: the PGIB and TA. To date, the PGIB is the largest education benefit program available to service members and veterans in terms of yearly spending. PGIB pays for a variety of education-related expenses and includes a living allowance that varies based on location. In some cases, service members can transfer their PGIB benefits to a spouse or child. In terms of overall generosity, the PGIB is, in most cases, considerably more valuable than its predecessor, the MGIB. The MGIB was flexible in that benefits were paid directly to the recipient, but it was more restrictive than the current bill in scope and value (Barr, 2013; Martorell and Bergman, 2013). Indeed, the PGIB is closer in spirit to the original GI Bill passed in 1944.

The main program supporting pursuit of higher education while serving is TA. Each service has a separate TA program and slightly different requirements, but the structure is similar: This benefit pays for the cost of tuition with per–credit hour and per-year limits. Service members use TA to attend school, generally on a part-time basis, while serving.

Together, these programs make up the majority of DoD and U.S. Department of Veterans Affairs (VA) expenditures on education benefits for service members and veterans today. There are numerous other programs that service members and veterans can access to further their education, but limiting the project focus to two large programs enabled us to assess program effectiveness and efficiency in a focused manner, while including the programs that make up the bulk of the spending in this area. Finally, administrative data are available on these programs; therefore, we can carry out our analyses at a granular level. Appendix A provides more detailed information on TA and the various GI Bills, as well as some information on the other education programs available to service members and veterans.

Overview of Research Approaches and Data Limitations

Understanding the level of knowledge, usage, and plans for usage at each point in a service member's career is key to observing the likely impact of the passage of the PGIB on recruitment and retention outcomes. For example, if recruits have little knowledge about PGIB benefits, then we should not expect to see a large impact of PGIB on recruitment. Similarly, the level of awareness about the details for transferring benefits to dependents would inform expectations about likely impacts of transferability on retention.

Figure 1.1 depicts the evolution of knowledge and use of education benefits over a military member's time of service. We posit that recruits acquire general knowledge about education benefits as they consider whether or not to join the service, and then gain knowledge over their careers, particularly as they develop and implement a usage plan. Knowledge can be facilitated by influencers like military recruiters or college counselors, by information and advertising campaigns sponsored by the military and other sources, and by peers who have used or plan to use their benefits. The level of knowledge about benefits can influence service member decisions at every decision point in the military career. These points range over the time of service and beyond. They include the point where recruits are considering whether or not to join, and whether or not they use the benefits. The points also include their decision to reenlist, and whether and how they use the benefit at each reenlistment point. The career trajectory framework also captures decisions about how military members use the benefits upon separation from service.

The green, purple, and orange boxes in Figure 1.1 depict the various data sources and approaches we utilized to assess service members' knowledge about and use of education benefits at each stage of their careers and beyond. We used both qualitative and quantitative approaches to assessing a vast amount of collected data. We summarize the data sources and methods used in the study below and present full information in each corresponding chapter of analysis.

Figure 1.1
Conceptual Framework for Education Benefits Decisionmaking Process

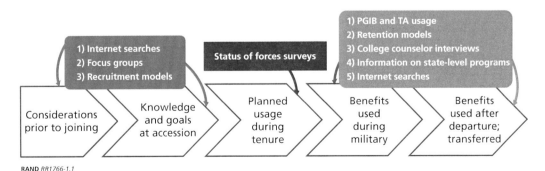

RAND RR1766-1.1

Qualitative Methods and Sources

The study draws upon a variety of qualitative data sources to understand service member knowledge about the level of education benefits available and details about the programs and plans for usage (if any) over the lifespan. We conducted a series of focus groups of new service members in the Delayed Entry Program (DEP) to identify service member knowledge around the time of accession. We collected and analyzed search terms related to education benefits programs using Google Analytics. To understand service member knowledge, usage, and planned usage of benefits during service, we analyzed questions from the Status of Forces (SOF) survey. To better understand service member knowledge and usage of benefits after separation from service, we conducted interviews with eight college counselors specializing in military students at colleges across the United States.

Quantitative Methods

Our quantitative analyses draw upon rich administrative data from the Defense Manpower Data Center (DMDC), the VA, each branch of the U.S. Armed Services, and other sources. We link databases from these agencies at the individual level and across time to develop a longitudinal database tracking all applicants for military service from 2002 to 2015, and capturing a range of information on characteristics of service members and their dependents at entry and at six-month intervals through separation from service or 2015. The data also capture detailed information on use of TA by the member and PGIB usage by the member and his or her dependents. We use this database to analyze the effects of PGIB passage on recruitment and retention, and to analyze the complementarities between the PGIB and TA programs using a variety of econometric approaches that we describe later. The particular analyses we conduct are informed by a set of hypotheses that we develop and refine using evidence from the qualitative results.[1]

Data Limitations

Despite the rich data at our disposal, evaluating our primary research questions using quantitative methods presents various difficulties because of the specifics of PGIB and the time period during which the bill was passed and enacted. First, the period of time covered in our study (2002–2015) was marked by a series of dramatic changes to the typical experiences of service members (for example, a substantial increase in the time spent deployed) and within the civilian economy (for example, the unemployment rate increased sharply in 2009). The passage of the PGIB occurred in the midst of these changes. During this same time frame, other recruiting and retention incentives (such as enlistment bonuses and selective reenlistment bonuses) were used

---

[1]   This study was reviewed and approved by RAND's Human Subjects Protection Committee, as well as by appropriate authorities within the Office of the Secretary of Defense.

quite heavily. For context, Figure 1.2 provides information on recruit quality and on civilian economic conditions. Specifically, Figure 1.2 demonstrates the sharp increase in the civilian unemployment rate that occurred during passage and enactment of the PGIB (recall that the bill was passed in 2008 and enacted in 2009). Over the entire period covered in Figure 1.2, recruit quality varied somewhat, but the general trend was toward increasing quality, and for much of the period recruit quality was quite high in historic terms.

Due to the many concurrent changes, separating the effects of education benefits poses significant empirical challenges. In our quantitative analyses, we employ several strategies to overcome these challenges. First, we compare service members' responses before and after the passage of the PGIB; we hold constant as many other factors as possible in these comparisons. Due to the many other factors changing over the time period, we also compare information on different groups of service members likely to value education benefits in different ways. For example, service members with dependents were likely to find more value in the potential to transfer the PGIB than service members without dependents. Also, a number of states provided education benefits to service members independently of the PGIB; we compare the responses of service

Figure 1.2
Recruit Quality and the Civilian Unemployment Rate, 2001–2014

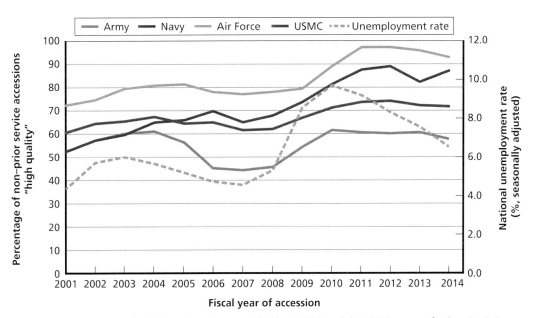

SOURCE: RAND NDRI analysis, based on data provided by DMDC and the U.S. Bureau of Labor Statistics.
NOTE: "High quality" = score of at least 50th percentile on the Armed Forces Qualification Test (AFQT) and high school diploma or equivalent credential.
RAND RR1766-1.2

members in three of these states (Illinois, Texas, and Wisconsin) to the responses of service members in similar states that lacked such programs.

More specifically, to empirically assess our research questions, we use five primary strategies: (1) interrupted time-series at the national level, (2) difference-in-differences for strategic differential responses across service member attributes, (3) difference-in-differences and triple difference estimators for regional analyses where we leverage states that already had similar education programs in place, (4) within-person pre-post analysis (fixed effects) for repeated choices that service members make, and (5) by-person regressions of decisions, the most weakly identified.

Organization of This Report

Chapter Two provides further context for the study by describing PGIB and TA benefits more fully. We also review relevant literature pertaining to decision factors, motivations, and propensity for joining the military. Chapter Three presents the analysis and findings pertaining to new recruits' perspectives of military education benefits, while Chapter Four presents the perspectives of college military and veteran student office personnel. Chapter Five examines the impact of the passage of the PGIB on recruitment and retention and assesses whether and how military personnel use both the TA and PGIB programs separately or together to further their education. Chapter Six looks into potential recruit, service member, and veterans' education benefit knowledge and usage with a combination of data and methods. Finally, Chapter Seven summarizes our findings and offers recommendations for USD(P&R) and DoD leaders more generally to consider going forward.

This work is supported by multiple appendices. Appendix A presents an overview of all education benefits available to service members and veterans. Appendix B presents an in-depth overview on the programs of study, TA and PGIB. Appendix C presents additional statistical and quantitative results from our study pertaining especially to retention. Appendix D offers more information on methods used on the Internet search queries. Appendix E presents our in-depth analysis of the SOF survey data.

CHAPTER TWO

Research on the Impact of Military Service and Education Benefits on Educational Attainment and Civilian Earnings

In this chapter, we provide a brief overview of the literature most relevant to this research. The literature on educational attainment and labor market outcomes is rich and well established; we describe this literature only briefly before focusing on research that emphasizes various aspects of educational benefits provided to service members.

Benefits and the Transition to the Civilian World

The positive relationship between educational attainment and labor market earnings is well established in the literature (see, among many, Card, 1999). In particular, those who complete a degree (high school, community college, or four-year college) have substantially higher earnings and more positive labor market outcomes (see, among many, Jaeger and Page 1996; Jepsen, Troske, and Coomes, 2014). Indeed, obtaining even minimal amounts of additional education raises long-term earnings, and educational benefits may have multigenerational effects. Specifically, there is evidence that even limited community college coursework leads to an increase in earnings that well exceeds the cost of attendance (Kane and Rouse, 1995). Examining an earlier benefit, the children of the service members who used the original GI Bill had a lower likelihood of being retained (and thus higher levels of educational attainment) than children of similar men who did not qualify for the benefit (Page, undated).

Enlisted service members enter the military during the time period when many young people instead attend postsecondary or trade schools. Thus, the educational attainment and civilian earnings of service members and veterans could be expected to follow different trajectories from those of more traditional students and workers. Recent research tracking earnings of those who did and did not enlist over a long horizon indicates that among enlisted service members, military service initially increases earnings by a substantial amount; the longer-term effect is also positive but somewhat smaller. Educational attainment appears to play some role in this relationship; enlistment delays college education but increases the likelihood of earning a two-year degree while decreasing the likelihood of earning a four-year degree (Loughran et al., 2011).[1] However, this research examined personnel eligible for the MGIB. A key characteristic of the MGIB was the necessity to opt (and pay) into the benefit during the first year of service. In contrast, service members may opt into the PGIB at any point throughout their careers after qualifying; also, the PGIB offers more generous benefits (Martorell and Bergman, 2013). For these reasons, the take-up rate may be higher, and the educational choices may differ, among service members who qualify for PGIB compared with earlier cohorts. Indeed, initial research suggests the PGIB not only increases enrollment and persistence, but veterans using the PGIB are likely to enroll at (relatively expensive) four-year institutions (Barr, 2013). This is linked to the structure of the benefit—the PGIB includes funds for tuition and fees but also funds for other living expenses. (The MGIB in contrast provided a single monthly payment to the student). Therefore, the MGIB incentivized users to choose inexpensive schools located in areas with relatively low costs of living, as the benefit amount did not depend on the cost of the school or the region. In contrast, the PGIB incentivizes the selection of more-expensive schools (up to the maximum benefit rates) and may incentivize locating in more expensive areas. This is likely to influence educational attainment. It is worth noting that other research finds somewhat different effects of education benefits on school choice; for example, Gilpin and Kofoed (2015) find that workers who have access to employer-based tuition assistance programs actually choose less expensive (and lower-quality) MBA programs. It is not clear how to compare these results with the incentives of the PGIB; employer-based tuition assistance programs may serve to encourage students to obtain additional education. The PGIB, and the MGIB, may have the same effect.

Finally, the PGIB is a complex benefit, in several respects. Although service members need not "opt in" to the benefit at an early point in their careers, transferring the benefit to a spouse or child must be completed prior to leaving the military. Given the 36-month limit, planning and optimal course taking are likely necessary to complete a degree within the benefit limits. Using TA and PGIB in concert may be useful in this regard, but especially complex. In some of the earliest research on the PGIB, veteran students expressed confusion about the options available to them and the amount of benefit eligibility, as well as concerns and frustrations over the ability to transfer credits (for example, those earned through military training or TA) (Steele et al., 2011).

Education Benefits—Evidence on Enlistment and Retention

The relationship between education benefits and enlistment/retention has not been ignored. For example, Simon, Negrusa, and Warner (2010) lay out a framework for

---

[1]   Research on earlier cohorts suggested that many who were drafted into military service has substantially *lower* earnings even ten to 20 years after service, suggesting that at least in an earlier era, military service had a relatively low payoff in the civilian sector; see Angrist, 1990.

evaluating the effects of military education benefits from the perspective of DoD; they include the effect on enlistment, on enlistment selection (change in quality of enlistees), and reenlistment.[2] Our analysis accords well with this framework.[3] These authors also find evidence that education benefits attract high-quality recruits.

The military as a whole is concerned with the total number of recruits within a fiscal year, but also with the quality of those recruits. A *high-quality* enlisted recruit is considered to be one with at least a high school diploma and better than average scores on the AFQT; these recruits have a better record of completing their initial term of service than other recruits (Buddin, 2005, among many others).[4] Education benefits have been shown to be attractive to high-quality recruits (Polich, Fernandez, and Orvis, 1982, among many others). Enlistment bonuses and other aspects of service have also been shown to influence potential recruits (see, e.g., Asch et al., 2010).

According to results from the University of Michigan's "Monitoring the Future" (MtF) project during the 1990s, high school students planning on continuing their education at a four-year college showed a desire to serve that was higher than their *expectation* to serve (Segal et al., 1999). In other words, students expressed a wish to serve but were not confident that they would be able to do so. For example, some might have worried about meeting various qualifications. In the 1999 Youth Attitude Tracking Study (YATS), getting money for college was one of the top six goal items that differentiated military service from civilian employment (Eighmey, 2006). These findings imply that education benefits could be a valuable tool for attracting recruits who are likely to meet the *high quality* definition. If those planning on furthering their education are open to serving in the military but do not see its benefit, programs such as the PGIB that could enable attendance at a more expensive—and presumably high-quality—institution could be effective. Barr (2015) finds that PGIB recipients attend relatively expensive schools.

In 2009, approximately 48 percent of recruits were over 20 years of age (Rostker, Klerman, and Zander-Cutugno, 2014). In the same study, it was found that "money for education" was more likely to be a primary motivation for joining among these late joiners than among recent high school graduates (87 percent of late joiners listed it as a primary motivation, while 80 percent of high school enlistees did so). This suggests that older recruits may be especially interested in educational opportunities afforded by enlistment.

---

[2]   Simon, Negrusa, and Warner (2010) also include the probability that a separated individual uses education benefits; see Martorell and Bergman (2013) for a more detailed analysis of Montgomery GI Bill benefits usage post-separation from military service.

[3]   Other research examines various aspects of this framework as well; for example, the effect of education benefits on reenlistment has been examined (Congressional Budget Office, 2006, among others), and the gains to the military from enlisting more skilled personnel for briefer periods (Asch, Kilburn, and Klerman, 1999).

[4]   There is no parallel definition of quality among officers.

The unique transfer aspect of the PGIB means that there is little relevant research, to date, on how this benefit is likely to affect retention. Using a combination of administrative data on sailors who received the Navy College Fund and survey data on stated intentions to reenlist, Schmitz and Moskowitz (2009) estimate a small overall negative effect on retention due to the passage of the PGIB, but a more substantial positive effect on stated intentions to reenlist in the future due to the ability to transfer the benefit. It is unclear how best to translate these particular stated intentions, but this research also suggests that intentions to reenlist are far more volatile than actual reenlistment rates; among those at the end of the first term, stated intentions suggested retention would decrease by 3 to 5 percentage points, but in fact the decrease was about 1 percentage point. This suggests that the actual increase in retention rates due to the transfer option will be quite small.

Finally, there is some research on TA. Previous research found that for at least two services (Navy and Marine Corps), a negative correlation existed between TA usage and reenlistment (Buddin and Kappur, 2005).[5] The cost-free accumulation of credits while on active duty was shown to encourage separation in order to complete the degree—an incentive that may be even higher with postseparation GI Bill benefits that cover most, if not all, of the remaining courses. However, it is important to note the program usage and reenlistment data used for this analysis were from 1997 and 1998, and no similar analysis has been conducted with more current data.

In general, the literature suggests that potential recruits consider education benefits valuable, but it is not clear how recruits weigh education benefits versus, for example, enlistment bonuses. There is also little information on how a benefit with a transfer option such as that offered by the PGIB is likely to affect retention.

Next, we discuss our qualitative findings based on focus groups of new service members and their knowledge of and plans to use education benefits.

---

[5] Garcia, Arkes, and Trost (2002) find a positive correlation between TA usage and retention in the Navy. However, it is not clear that they adequately control for time in the Navy, or for the factors that may influence use of TA.

CHAPTER THREE
Perspectives of New Recruits on Military Education Benefits

To understand the role of military education benefits in service member decisionmaking, it is important to have some information about what service members know about military education benefits, when service members learn about various aspects of the benefits available to them, and whether service members plan to use their benefits. For military education benefits to have an impact on recruitment and retention, individuals must be aware of the benefits available to them at the time of decisionmaking and must have an interest in using these benefits. In addition, the analytic models used to estimate the impacts of military education benefits typically require assumptions about the knowledge individuals have of their benefits. For example, these models might assume that individuals understand specific details about the value of their benefits and variation in benefits across time, across programs, or across geographic regions.

Conversations with service members can help to shed light on what is known about education benefits and how individuals plan to use them. By speaking with new recruits, individuals preparing to enlist in the military, we were able to better understand what is known at the time of enlistment and the degree to which information on military education benefits may have affected enlistment decisions. While it is important to understand how knowledge of military education benefits evolves over time and, thus, how it may play a role in later decisions to continue service and reenlist, we were unable to arrange focus groups with individuals nearing reenlistment for this study. Therefore, the findings in this chapter focus on new recruits—both their level of knowledge about education benefits and how they made the decision to enlist in the military. Finally, while we purposefully included members from across the country and from each branch of the armed services so that the information we gathered would be as representative of the population of new recruits nationally as possible, we do not claim to ensure that our sample is completely representative.

Methodology

To learn about the perspectives of new recruits, we conducted sixteen 45-minute focus groups with service members across all four branches—the Army, Navy, Air Force, and Marine Corps. We selected four U.S. cities—Baltimore, Maryland; Los Angeles, California; Richmond, Virginia; and San Antonio, Texas—and contacted recruiters at the recruiting stations in regions around these cities to assist in selecting focus group participants from recruits currently in the DEP. Table 3.1 indicates the total number of focus groups and participants by military branch.[1] None of the participants had attended boot camp, though the timing of when they first initiated the recruitment process ranged widely across individuals. Some individuals had been given a ship date and job assignment at the time of the discussion, while others had not. Our focus groups included individuals planning to join the enlisted ranks, and participants varied by age, race/ethnicity, gender, and education level.

Each focus group began with an explanation of the study and an informed consent process. We developed a protocol that included 14 questions that touched on several issues: the timing and reasoning behind deciding to join the military, awareness of military education benefits, knowledge about the specific conditions of the PGIB and TA programs, source of information on military education benefits, and plans to use military education benefits. We took detailed notes of the discussions and conducted analysis of focus group notes to identify key themes that emerged from the discussions around each of these issues.

Table 3.1
Focus Groups and Participants by Region and Service Branch

City	Air Force Focus Groups	Air Force New Recruits	Army Focus Groups	Army New Recruits	Marines Focus Groups	Marines New Recruits	Navy Focus Groups	Navy New Recruits	Total Focus Groups	Total New Recruits
Baltimore, Md.	1	11	0	0	1	9	0	0	2	20
Los Angeles, Calif.	1	9	2	15	1	10	2	15	6	49
Richmond, Va.	1	16	0	0	1	8	2	33	4	57
San Antonio, Texas	1	12	2	17	1	10	0	0	4	39
Total	4	48	4	32	4	37	4	48	16	165

----

[1] Focus groups with Army and Navy recruits were held in only two cities due to constraints on when these focus groups could be scheduled.

In several areas, we were able to calculate exact proportions of participants who provided certain responses because we collected responses from all participants. This includes information on why the recruits decided to join the military, for which we went around the room allowing every participant to respond, and information on college plans and reasons for planning to attend or not attend, for which responses were collected from all participants by pencil and paper. We did not systematically collect information across respondents regarding knowledge of benefits and plan for use (but instead allowed new recruits to volunteer information), so we are limited to more general statements on the pervasiveness of knowledge or perspectives on these topics. Also, we assured participants that they could skip any questions they did not wish to answer; some did not answer questions about knowledge of benefits and plans for benefit use. Because our sample is not necessarily representative of all new recruits and because we did not systematically collect information on some questions, we often do not provide specific percentages of new recruits who agree with statements (such percentages could suggest a higher level of precision than our framework can support).

Findings

Recruitment Decisions

We asked recruits to describe their decisions to join the military, including when they first started thinking about joining, why they decided to join, and whom they talked with as they were making their decisions. Participants varied widely in when they reported starting to think about joining the military. Approximately a third of new recruits in our focus groups reported that they'd always wanted to join, or had thought about joining from a relatively young age. Another third of recruits recalled early high school, a time when many students are contemplating future education and employment plans, as the time when they first started thinking about joining the military. The remaining third of recruits reported a more recent decision to join the military, toward the end of high school or after struggling with college or employment after high school. There were no notable patterns in the timing of decisionmaking about joining the military by service branch, geographic location, or gender.

Recruits cited a wide variety of reasons for joining the military. The most commonly cited reasons for joining were employment-related, including getting an immediate job and getting training and experience for other jobs in the future; at least one participant in every focus group mentioned a need for a job or career preparation as a reason for joining. One recruit specifically mentioned the value of the military in providing a career rather than just a job. Benefits were the second–most commonly mentioned reason for joining the military, mentioned in every focus group. Education benefits were one of the more frequently mentioned benefits; all but two of the focus groups specifically highlighted education benefits as a reason for joining the military.

There was a clear pattern in responses by service branch, with new recruits to the Air Force, Army, and Navy more likely to mention benefits as a driving factor, relative to the Marines. Related to education, new recruits mentioned their desire to avoid incurring college-related debt as a reason for joining the military and pursuing education using earned benefits. In five of our focus groups, recruits mentioned that they had already incurred college-related debt prior to enlistment, and questions were raised in two of the focus groups about whether loan repayment programs were still in place. On the other hand, some new recruits had a substantially different orientation to education; these recruits reported deciding to join the military after struggling in school (high school or college). In nine of our 16 focus groups, we had at least one recruit respond that the choice to enter the military was as an alternative to college.

Other commonly cited drivers of recruitment beyond employment- and education-related considerations include maintaining the family tradition, being able to contribute to something bigger, and patriotism. In approximately half of our focus groups, particularly those with Marine recruits, we heard of the elitism of being part of a select group, the physical challenge, and discipline as being important reasons for joining the military. In two focus groups, we heard about the ability to become a citizen and opportunities for travel, and in three of the focus groups, recruits mentioned adventure as reasons for considering military service.

As new recruits were considering joining the military, they most commonly reported having spoken with family and friends about their decision; every focus group included recruits who spoke with friends and family. The majority of recruits across every focus group also mentioned interactions with recruiters, and these interactions were more commonly initiated by the recruits than the recruiter according to our focus group participants. Focus group participants from the Air Force were more likely to report that recruiters were challenging to establish contact with; Marine recruits were more likely to report that the recruiter initiated contact. In more than half of our groups we heard that recruits had other important influencers in the decisionmaking process, including teachers, ROTC instructors, neighbors, and significant others.

Awareness of Benefit Programs

While many of the recruits we spoke with cited education benefits and the ability to pay for college as important considerations in joining the military, they tended to refer to these benefits in a general way and did not specifically cite details of the programs or describe plans for using them. When we probed further on what programs came to mind when we mentioned education benefits, at least one recruit in each of our focus groups mentioned the GI Bill, with recruits in two of our focus groups specifically highlighting distinctions between the PGIB and the MGIB. Overall, approximately three-quarters of the participants in our focus groups seemed to be familiar with the GI Bill programs. It was more challenging for recruits to come up with programs beyond the GI Bill programs. In five of the 16 focus groups, there were no other programs mentioned, and in the 11 focus groups where other programs were mentioned, typically fewer than half of recruits were aware of other programs. When recruits cited other education benefit programs, they mentioned loan repayment, the TA program, ROTC, credits for military service, and state programs like the Hazelwood Act in Texas. Across all of our focus groups, less than a quarter of recruits were familiar with the TA program.

Knowledge of the Post-9/11 GI Bill Program

In order to understand more about the knowledge recruits have regarding military education benefit programs, we asked new recruits about the specific details of the PGIB program, including (1) how service members qualify, (2) who can actually use the benefits, (3) when the benefits can be used, (4) what the benefits cover, and (5) whether the amount of benefits changes based on time in the military and other factors. At least one of the recruits in each focus group was able to provide some specific details on the PGIB program, though many recruits did not appear to be particularly confident in the accuracy of their knowledge, and the information was sometimes conflicting and/or inaccurate. We observed that the recruits able to speak to details of the PGIB program were often the same recruits who had prior college experience and/or mentioned education benefits as a primary driver in decisions to enlist. In other cases, individuals well versed in the program's features cited prior family experience with benefits as the source of their knowledge. On the other hand, many recruits were direct about their lack of knowledge on the program; 12 of our 16 focus groups included recruits who mentioned they didn't know much. One recruit noted that he'd "learn more about the specifics when he actually needed to use them." The Air Force focus groups were more likely to include a number of recruits who could provide detailed information on the specifics of PGIB, followed by participants in the Navy and Army focus groups, where awareness levels varied across focus groups, but at least one or two individuals in each group did seem to have some detailed knowledge.

With regard to qualification for PGIB benefits, most of the recruits who offered detailed knowledge mentioned that this required active duty, though one recruit noted that Reservists were eligible in some cases for the benefits. There was substantial uncertainty about how long a service member needed to be on active duty to qualify for benefits. A 90-day enlistment period was mentioned in one of the focus groups, while enlistment periods of one year, three years and four years were also suggested as requirements to receive PGIB benefits (each was mentioned in two groups). There was also uncertainty about whether the amount of the benefit increased with time in the military, with new recruits equally likely to report that that they did and did not think benefit amounts depend on time in service (among those who volunteered a response to our probing on this question). One recruit suggested that each new contract might be tied to an additional PGIB benefit. So while new recruits had a general sense that there may be requirements for time in service, there was not a good sense of the specific details of phased-in benefit levels between 90 days and 36 months of service.

The new recruits we spoke with suggested other potential restrictions on qualification for the PGIB beyond time in service that varied in accuracy. One recruit mentioned the requirement that service members be honorably discharged. Another recruit reported (inaccurately) that individuals might need to be at a certain rank to qualify. The requirement to maintain certain grades in courses was mentioned by participants in three of the focus groups. Focus group participants had mixed views on the ability to use benefits while still in the military: Approximately half of the groups had a participant who mentioned PGIB benefits could be used while in the military, while the other half of focus groups had participants who were unsure or did not think the benefits could be used while still in service. Several recruits mentioned requirements to pay into the system to receive benefits; however, others in the two groups where this was mentioned suggested that this was specific to the MGIB and did not apply to the PGIB.

The ability to transfer benefits to dependents was raised in all but one of the groups we spoke with (prior to our probing specifically on this feature), though there were a number of recruits within each focus group who did not seem to be aware of transferability. We did not probe on the specifics of transfer, including service requirements, qualifying dependents, and benefit levels, and none of the recruits specifically mentioned the requirement of reenlistment for transfer of benefits. At the end of the focus groups, when we provided information on PGIB benefits, some recruits did appear surprised to hear about the reenlistment requirement.

New recruits were somewhat uncertain about what costs were covered by the PGIB and the amount of benefits available. Recruits in each of our focus groups reported knowledge that the benefits cover the bulk of tuition. Knowledge that PGIB benefits include housing costs was somewhat more limited; only ten of the 16 focus groups had recruits who volunteered housing costs as included prior to our probes specifically asking about these costs. In two of our focus groups, participants shared conflicting opinions about whether housing costs were covered under the PGIB. Recruits in six of the focus groups mentioned that textbooks were also covered under the program. When we asked new recruits about the total size of benefits, a few provided estimates of $70,000 to $80,000 total, but most recruits did not report having a good sense of the value of the benefits. None of the recruits expressed awareness of the indexing of total benefits to public college tuition or basic allowance for housing, and no one mentioned that total benefits might vary by location. Recruits in three of the groups across different services inquired about using GI Bill benefits to pay off existing student debt.

New recruits reported having learned about their benefits from a range of different sources. The most commonly mentioned sources of information on the PGIB program were the Internet and recruiters, each mentioned in at least two-thirds of our focus groups. We did not specifically ask the focus groups about the quality of the information they receive, though one recruit specifically noted that he found the information available on the PGIB at the VA website confusing. And while many of the new recruits portrayed recruiters as a valuable source of information, recruits in two of our focus groups reported they were skeptical of the accuracy of and motivation for the information they received from recruiters. New recruits mentioned several other sources including family, friends, and high school staff (each raised in at least three focus groups). New recruits often noted that their family and friends who served as sources of information were prior users of GI Bill benefits.

Knowledge of the Tuition Assistance Program

Just as new recruits were less likely to be aware of the TA program relative to the PGIB program, they were substantially less likely to be aware of the details of the program. More than one-third of the focus groups involved no discussion of the awareness of TA program details because no one was aware of the program. On the other hand, in one Air Force focus group all but two of the participants had heard of TA. New recruits to the Marines were particularly unlikely to be aware of the details of the TA program; only one group involved substantial discussion of TA. There was some confusion between the TA program and the loan repayment program, with recruits from two of our focus groups suggesting that TA benefits could be used to cover costs from previous loans.

Among the few recruits who reported awareness of details on the TA program, approximately one-third were unsure of what was required to qualify, while the rest were aware that this program was restricted to service members. One recruit mentioned that he believed there was a requirement to have completed basic training, but otherwise the focus group participants did not appear to be aware of any service requirements to receive TA benefits. Another recruit mentioned the requirement that service members would have to "pay back" the benefits if they did achieve a certain grade.

New recruits aware of the TA program generally reported that it covered tuition only, although focus group participants in two of the focus groups suggested it might also cover books. The reported size of TA benefits varied widely across recruits who mentioned knowledge of the program's details. Several recruits noted that the benefits covered only a portion of total tuition costs, while others reported that all costs were covered. There were also differing opinions on whether the benefit was determined as a yearly allowance or a total amount. One focus group participant mentioned that benefits were "a few thousand per year" but couldn't remember the exact amount, while another provided a figure of $4,000 per year. Two recruits cited knowledge of $10,000 (unclear whether total or per-year) for the TA benefit, and another mentioned $80,000 total.

In the focus groups where new recruits mentioned knowledge of the TA program, recruits were most likely to cite their primary informational source as being a recruiter and/or information distributed by the military during enlistment. Recruits mentioned the Internet as an informational resource for TA in three of our focus groups, and one new recruit mentioned her parents as a source of information.

Plans to Use Military Education Benefits

We first asked new recruits specifically about their plans to attend college. Approximately one-third of the recruits we spoke with mentioned prior experience with college; some had exited without completing a degree while others reported having completed bachelor's degrees, and in a few cases master's degrees. Regardless of past education, the vast majority reported plans to attend college in the future. Air Force recruits were the most likely to report plans to attend college (96 percent), followed by Army and Navy recruits (87 to 88 percent), and then Marine recruits (76 percent). Those who did not report plans to attend college generally cited a dislike of school or the lack of relevance for their desired career as the reasons for making this decision. Among those who reported plans to attend college, the reasons for doing so varied across participants; they included employment-related reasons, a desire to earn more money, and a desire to learn more. We also asked focus group participants about perceived barriers to college enrollment. Recruits strongly emphasized cost as the primary barrier to enrollment, with more than three-quarters of recruits reporting cost to be among the top barriers among the options given. While recruits did note other barriers as playing a role (e.g., difficulty of coursework, lack of time, lack of relevance to job), cost was much more likely to be reported as the most important barrier.

After learning about the college plans of our new recruits, we inquired about their plans to use military education benefits. More than 90 percent of our new recruits reported plans to use military education benefits. While most of the recruits reported that some portion of the benefits would be used to support their own educational costs, participants in more than half of our focus groups reported plans to transfer benefits to dependents. When we probed on the specifics of the plans to use military education benefits, relatively few recruits offered detailed plans. We found that older recruits, especially those with prior college experience, were the most likely to provide details on their plans for use, and the participants with specific plans were typically those who had been able to provide details on the program requirements. In two of our Navy focus groups, recruits expressed an interest in remaining on active duty long enough to qualify for transfer of PGIB benefits to their dependents. Among the few recruits who volunteered specifics, most reported plans to use benefits both while enlisted and after leaving military service, while just two recruits with detailed plans mentioned holding off on using benefits until after completing service. Two recruits reported plans to use benefits for both undergraduate and graduate degrees, and recruits in three of our focus groups mentioned plans for using the benefits to prepare for particular careers.

Summary

Our conversations with new recruits suggest that the existence of military education benefits does play a prominent role in some enlistment decisions, and the majority of new recruits do plan to use their benefits. However, knowledge of benefit programs varies across new recruits, and most have limited knowledge about the specifics of the PGIB and TA programs. This suggests that a general awareness of benefits, rather than consideration of specific restrictions or benefit components, is likely to be driving enlistment decisions. For this reason, it is not clear that we should expect a large enlistment response after the passage of the PGIB. The few recruits who were well informed about military education benefits appeared to be older, more likely to have prior experience with college, more likely to be female, and less likely to be entering the Marines. Recruits who were aware of the details of various benefit programs and have more specific plans for using the benefits may be more likely to respond to specific benefit changes in decisionmaking about enlistment. Next, we present information on the perspectives of military and veteran student offices, learned through a small number of targeted interviews.

.

CHAPTER FOUR

Perspectives of College Military and Veteran Student Offices on Military Education Benefits

To develop clear and well-informed hypotheses about the likely impact of PGIB passage on enlistment and retention, it is important to understand the role of military education benefits on service member decisionmaking, including the impact that these benefits have on people's decisions to serve in the military and the ways in which benefits are used in practice. It is useful to learn about the decisionmaking process when service members initially join the military, as well as their decisions to reenlist and to use their education benefits while enlisted or after separating from the military. While the focus group discussions with new recruits were useful in assessing the impact of military education benefits on recruiting decisions, we also conducted interviews with advisors at a small number of college military and veteran student offices to examine later-stage knowledge and decisionmaking. Specifically, we wanted to learn more about service members' and veterans' knowledge of their military education benefits, how these benefits are used, and how they might impact decisionmaking around education and military enlistment. Due to the small number of interviews, these results should be interpreted with caution. This chapter details findings from these interviews with advisors at college military and veteran offices.

Methodology

We conducted eight semistructured phone interviews with student advisors in military and veteran student offices at colleges across the United States. Colleges were selected based on their high share of military students, and interviewees at each school were identified based on a web-based search of military student resources and contacts available on campus. We chose a range of different types of colleges to ensure that our discussions were not limited to certain student populations and accounted for a range of different users of military education benefits. Table 4.1 provides some information on the colleges. The institutions we sampled included two-year and four-year institutions and institutions with different funding models. The location of institutions varied, and some institutions were primarily online programs, while others offer on-site and online opportunities. In some cases we identified colleges for interviews based on high levels

Table 4.1
Interviews and Participating Colleges, by Region and Type of College

College	Midwest	Northeast	South	West	National/Online	Total
Public, 2-Year	0	0	1	1	0	2
Public, 4-Year	1	1	0	1	0	3
Private, for-profit	0	0	0	0	2	2
Private, not-for-profit	1	0	0	0	0	1
Total	2	1	1	2	2	8

of GI Bill and TA benefit use according to available data to ensure that the veteran offices were among those most familiar with military education benefit users. Therefore, although we spoke to a small number of advisors, they had interacted with many military-connected students.

Each interview began with an explanation of the study and an informed consent process. We developed a protocol that included 13 questions that touched on several issues: the awareness of military education benefits, knowledge about the specific conditions of the PGIB and TA programs, source of information on military education benefits, use of military education benefits and impact on recruitment decisions, and academic performance of military students. We took detailed notes of the discussions and conducted analysis of interview notes to identify key themes that emerged from the discussions around each of these issues. Given the qualitative nature and small number of our interviews, our data are not generalizable to the general population of college advisors nationally, and we can make only general statements about the observations made by the population we interviewed. Additionally, we note that our interviews were with schools that had veteran advisors, and not all schools responded to our requests for interviews. Therefore, these schools could represent a best-case scenario in terms of veteran support—or they could be unrepresentative in some other manner. Unfortunately, there is no single, inclusive database on veteran advisors that would allow us to determine the extent to which our sample is representative of all schools. Because our sample may not be generalizable, we do not describe our results in quantitative terms.

Findings

Awareness and Knowledge of the Post-9/11 GI Bill and Tuition Assistance Programs

To understand more about the knowledge that military students have regarding military education benefit programs, we asked advisors in military and veteran student offices about the students at their institutions and their level of knowledge with respect to (1) how service members qualify for military education benefits, (2) who can actually use the benefits, (3) when the benefits can be used, (4) what the benefits cover, and (5) whether the amount of benefits changes based on time in the military and other factors. We also asked about the sources of information on military education benefits for students who are service members or veterans.

Interviewees we spoke with at each of the eight programs suggested that PGIB benefits are complex and can be difficult to understand for many students, particularly those who have not previously attended college or used any kind of military education benefits. When prompted to describe the state of students' knowledge about their benefits, advisors explained that frequently, veterans arrive at their schools with some basic knowledge about their benefits and an understanding that they are eligible to receive something, but that there is a lack of detailed understanding among many about the specifics of their benefits and eligibility. With regard to the specifics of the PGIB, advisors in each of the eight programs reported that some students were not aware of the 36-month time frame for use of the benefits. Transferability of benefits was mentioned as one of the more frequently discussed topics with military and veteran students by interviewees at three of the programs we spoke with. Interviewees suggested that many did not understand the details regarding eligibility for transfer, and advisors at two colleges noted disappointment among uninformed veterans when they found out they had missed the window to register for transfer of their benefits. Advisors at more than half of the programs we spoke with also mentioned a lack of knowledge among some service members and veterans about service commitment rules, benefit amounts, and the inclusion of housing allowance in benefits. On the other hand, advisors in three of our interviews mentioned that many veterans are well aware of the existence of housing benefits and may have chosen to attend college primarily to receive the housing benefits, as opposed to having a clear interest in achieving educational credentials.[1]

According to our interviewees, military students generally appear to be more knowledgeable about their TA program benefits than they are about their PGIB benefits. Interviewees from six of the eight programs suggested that military students are well informed about TA programs, and two interviewees mentioned that the quality of education centers on military bases has contributed to active-duty military students being well informed about their TA program benefits. However, there are some gaps in knowledge in some areas; for example, one interviewee mentioned that some students are unaware that TA does not cover fees, and are in for a "rude awakening" when they enroll in college and learn that they will receive a bill. Across all of the programs we spoke with, college advisors reported that they provide relatively little assistance around information and registration for TA relative to their work with students on the PGIB. TA benefits appear to be handled mostly by the military service branches in conjunction with college administrative or registrar's offices. Consequently, the advi-

---

[1]   While some of the advisors' responses could indicate a lack of knowledge among dependents, other comments clearly reflected a perception that service members or veterans lacked a detailed understanding of their benefits.

sors at the eight colleges in our sample reported that they were primarily interacting with PGIB students.

In addition to PGIB and TA, advisors in each of the military and veteran student offices we spoke with provide information and assistance to students on other sources of financial support, including federal, state, and institutional aid and other military and veteran programs. One advisor noted that the availability of a range of other benefits for specific veteran populations might add to veterans' general confusion about military education benefits. However, the majority of the advisors we spoke with pointed out that most military and veteran students attending their institution are not thinking carefully about the trade-offs between uses of various funding sources and how they might maximize their use of military benefit programs. As a result, advisors play an important role in talking with individuals about these trade-offs. Advisors at four of the eight programs we spoke with reported encouraging military benefit users to use TA benefits to the degree possible while still enlisted and to use PGIB benefits only when other resources were not available. Advisors in three of the interviews reported that they have been strongly advising students against the usage of PGIB benefits while on active duty and to instead preserve their benefits for use after they leave the military, either for themselves or for their family members.

As well as from college military and veteran student offices, service members and veterans receive information from other sources. Advisors from three of the colleges noted that current DoD transition programs play a role in educating service members about their education benefits. However, advisors in two of our interviews suggested that these programs are perceived as inadequate in providing transitioning service members with the clear, personalized, and timely information they need to make informed decisions about benefit use. One advisor explained that the information is not presented in a way that allows them to grasp the full complexity of resources available. Another advisor suggested that some service members may have difficulty fully processing the large volume of complex information about education benefits to make informed decisions until the issues are made concrete, and they actually gain experience in using them.

In addition to transition programs, two of the programs we spoke with reported that several websites also served as informational resources, but that the sites are typically not user-friendly and carry too much information that is not organized in a way that is particularly useful for the target population. Military peer networks have also contributed to increased awareness of and interest in educational resources, with half of our program interviewees reporting that the most common way that new military students initially learn about their institution and how to enroll and use their educational benefits there is through their military and veteran peers who have already enrolled at the institution. However, one advisor noted that PGIB benefits in particular are highly individual and context-specific, and thus relying on other people's experiences might cause them to be misinformed. In response to the limited information service members and veterans are receiving about military education benefits from other resources, several of the colleges have substantially expanded the resource centers on their campuses and have started to provide more-active guidance on the use of military education benefits, particularly PGIB.[2]

One interesting observation we made during our interviews was that while all colleges served a mix of active-duty and veteran students, the discussion of benefit knowledge and use largely focused on one population or the other. We attribute this to two factors: (1) some of the colleges we interviewed are contracted TA providers, thus catering specifically to active-duty military students; and (2) the community colleges we spoke to mentioned that many active-duty military students will shy away from attending colleges that charge both tuition and fees, because fees are not covered under TA benefits.[3]

Use of Military Education Benefits and College Enrollment

While our new recruit focus groups provided some forward-looking predictions about whether they would potentially use their military education benefits, the advisors we interviewed were able to provide additional details about the actual use of benefits. Accordingly, we asked about the mix of financial resources used to pay for college education, potential challenges that military students are facing with regard to the usage of military education benefits, and the impact of benefits on their ability to succeed in and ultimately complete their academic programs.

Advisors from each of the eight programs we spoke with reported that military and veteran students often used a mix of financial resources to cover the costs of higher education. According to the interviewees, many veteran students and all military students are working and can therefore use income to supplement military education benefits. In addition, the majority of advisors we spoke with reported that they strongly encourage all students to apply for other federal and institutional benefits to supplement their military benefits. In line with the advice of advisors, two interviewees mentioned that active-duty service members often choose to use their TA benefits prior to tapping into PGIB benefits. One advisor remarked that more and more students are trying to get at least one degree while on active duty and have the ability to use TA. However, some students do use their PGIB benefits to supplement TA, as some col-

---

[2]   For example, one college located near a large military base reported providing regular workshops to both students and nonstudents in the community to promote financial literacy and inform individuals about military benefits. Another institution described a three-stage life-cycle support program that extends far beyond assistance with military education benefits and includes active outreach to service members to assist with applications, assistance with integration into college life, training of faculty on military and veteran student needs, and a variety of services to facilitate transitions into civilian employment.

[3]   Military dependents are a third group of military-connected students. While our interview questions focused on students who are current or former military members, it is possible that some advisors' comments were influenced by their interactions with military dependents.

lege costs cannot be covered by TA benefits (e.g., fees). Advisors at two of the institutions suggested that cuts or limitations to the TA program have led to an even greater number of active-duty military students relying on their PGIB benefits while still in service. Advisors at three of the colleges we spoke with suggested use of PGIB to supplement TA was an inefficient use of benefits because the service members were typically taking only a few courses but eating up valuable time in the 36-month window for PGIB use.

Ultimately, one aspect that advisors across all eight colleges agreed upon was that military education benefits drive college enrollment among military students. Advisors at one institution stated that the increase in TA coverage from 75 percent of tuition to 100 percent of tuition in 2002 has nearly doubled college enrollment among active-duty military personnel, and they expressed concern about the recent cuts in TA program benefits. Nevertheless, they also suggested that the complex nature of benefits imposes new challenges on the VA as well as on military student advisors at colleges in ensuring that military students are properly set up to maximize their benefits and to complete their academic programs. Military and veteran students typically had to rely on a mix of TA and PGIB benefits, as well as federal financial aid, to complete their programs according to advisors, and advisors at three of the colleges suggested that students often had difficulty completing their studies in a timely manner before their education benefits were exhausted.

Housing benefits included in the PGIB were referenced as a specific driver in college enrollment for certain students. Advisors at two of the colleges hypothesized that while many students would probably not go to college otherwise, they opted to do so because they could not find employment following their service and thus signed up for an academic program to receive a housing allowance. Yet advisors had conflicting opinions on the use of basic allowance for housing (BAH) benefits; advisors at two other colleges suggested that although military and veteran students might initially enroll in college for financial reasons, many become engaged in their education after they enroll and end up gaining valuable knowledge and skills in college. As one advisor described it, military education benefits are one of the very few ways for someone living from paycheck to paycheck to afford going to college.

College Experiences

Most military students, both veteran and active duty, face many of the challenges common to adult learner populations. They have a dual burden of work and class assignments, and they are often older than the average student, especially at traditional four-year colleges. Advisors at six of the colleges we spoke with reported that military and veteran students were comparable to other students at their institutions in terms of college readiness, while advisors at two colleges suggested military and veteran students might be somewhat more college-ready on average. One advisor noted that some professors tended to prefer having military students in their classes due to their discipline, work ethic, strong goal-orientation and high levels of maturity. Another advisor reported that while very few military students arrive on campus with college readiness in all subject areas, this was noted as a common problem for many students, regardless of military experience, at the institutions in question.

In terms of program length, college advisors across our eight colleges stated that while some military students opt to pursue four-year degrees, others first enroll in certificate or associate's degree programs. Interviewees cited several reasons for pursuing lower-level credentials: one interviewee suggested that some students might find the idea of a four-year college intimidating; two other interviewees mentioned that students are trying to use their TA benefits to complete a useful job-related credential while on active duty so that they can save their PGIB benefits for family members. However, advisors at two of the colleges also reported that some students have completed multiple degrees using military education benefits, including graduate degrees. Three of the advisors mentioned that the choice of major may vary by service branch and active versus veteran status. According to one interviewee, while on active duty, students often try to select majors that correspond directly to their field of service within the military, potentially due to the high degree of direct applicability to their day-to-day assignments. Advisors across the eight colleges suggested that law-enforcement and homeland security programs such as cybersecurity were among the most popular for both active-duty and veteran students. One advisor noted an increasing interest in STEM education and physical therapy among military and veteran students. For veterans, advisors were more likely to describe majors in business administration, accounting, and finance.

With regard to persistence and completion rates, advisors at three of the institutions reported that military students tended to fall behind other students due to the time and capacity constraints imposed by their active-duty military service assignments. In addition, advisors at two of the colleges mentioned that military and veteran students often struggled with the unstructured nature of the college environment and the fact that they had to plan their own schedules and keep track of their benefits. According to interviewees, depending on the academic program, some students are able to complete at least an associate's degree while in service, while others, particularly those studying in STEM-related areas, take longer to complete their studies. Advisors at two of the colleges suggested that military students should think very carefully about their choice of college and should consider the use of military service credits to further their academic careers.

We asked college advisors to elaborate on the ways in which they support military students. It's important to note that most of the colleges participating in our study were selected based on their large share of military students, and it can thus be presumed that these colleges have developed suitable strategies to guide and advise military students and to help them succeed. Interviewees reported that their efforts were focused on reducing the cost of college, facilitating the transition from a military to a college environment, and maximizing the use of military education benefits. Outside of military benefits counseling, interviewees mentioned assisting with in-state tuition for all military students, job placement programs, programs to facilitate transferring military credits, and enhanced academic and personal counseling.

Summary

Although our interviewees are not representative of all military and veteran student office administrators, their experiences are useful to consider in thinking about how veterans and service members use their benefits and the level of information they have when they do so. This information is crucial to help us develop informed hypotheses about the likely impact of PGIB passage on recruitment and particularly retention. The interviewed student advisors at eight colleges across the United States are playing an important role in supporting decisionmaking around the use of military education benefits. Advisors suggested that while military and veteran students are generally aware that they have military education benefits, they lack detailed knowledge about the underlying procedures and requirements, particularly in the case of the PGIB. With regards to academic achievement, advisors agreed that military students are performing similarly to other students. Nonetheless, student advisors also emphasized that some students are finding it difficult to adjust to a civilian college environment and to effectively manage both time and funds. Similarly, many students are not thinking strategically about how to utilize their various benefits and combine them with other sources of support (such as Federal Student Loans and Financial Aid) to maximize their educational pursuits. According to the advisors we interviewed, the complex nature of PGIB benefits, along with the limited guidance from government agencies, present a substantial challenge to veteran students; current active-duty military students using TA program benefits seem to be generally well prepared and informed by the education offices on military bases. In the next chapter, we present our estimates of the impact of the PGIB on recruiting and retention, based on administrative data sources.

CHAPTER FIVE

Empirical Strategies and Results

The goal of this chapter is to empirically estimate the impact of the passage of the PGIB on recruitment and retention and assess whether and how military personnel use both the TA and PGIB programs separately or together to further their education. We begin by describing the data sources we draw upon and how we link them at the individual level and across time to build our analytic data set. Next, we provide some information on the overall usage of the PGIB, and of TA. We describe our general quantitative hypotheses and the types of econometric methods we draw upon to assess them. We then present the results of our quantitative models. We conclude this chapter with a general summary of the quantitative findings.

Data

Our study draws upon a number of unique administrative data sets from the DMDC, the VA, and the individual Services (Army, Navy, Air Force, Marine Corps). In this section, we describe each of these primary data sets, and how we link them at the individual level over time to create an analytic data set that tracks the 2001–2014 cohorts of military accessions from the time they visit a U.S. Military Entrance and Processing Command (MEPCOM) station until 2014, or when they separate from military service. The file captures detailed information on service members as well as some information on their dependents at the time of application, at various points during their military career, and (for the PGIB usage data) a snapshot in the fall of 2015, composed primarily of after-service observations. We merge available information on each service member's usage and/or transfer of PGIB benefits, as well as usage of TA.

The specific administrative data sets that our study draws upon include

1. *The Work Experience File (WEX)* is a database built from DMDC's Active Duty Personnel Data System File and the Reserve Component Common Personnel Data System File that includes career information for all military personnel who served on or after September 30, 1990. We use WEX to capture individual-level data on date of entry, service (Army, Navy, Air Force, Marine Corps), compo-

nent (active versus reserve), promotions, pay grade, military occupation, and unit assignment over time for all members joining the service after 2000.[1]

2. *The MEPCOM File* is a database maintained by DMDC that captures key information taken when service members are processed for military service. We draw upon the MEPCOM file to capture demographic information (race/ ethnicity, gender, and age), the applicant's home state, educational status, and the percentile score on the AFQT for all applicants for military service.

3. *The Active Duty Pay File (ADPF)* is a database maintained by DMDC that contains detailed longitudinal information on military payments to service members in the active component. We use the ADPF to capture some detailed information on education-related payments to service members in the active component.

4. *The Reserve Pay File (RPF)* is a database maintained by DMDC that contains detailed longitudinal information on military payments to service members in the reserve component. We use the ADPF to capture some detailed information on education-related payments to service members in the reserve components.

5. *The Defense Enrollment Eligibility Reporting System (DEERS)* is a database maintained by DMDC that contains information on all service-connected individuals eligible for military benefits, such as the TRICARE health benefit. Because service members use DEERS to register their dependents as beneficiaries of military benefits, DEERS allowed us to collect longitudinal and detailed information on family characteristics, including marriage and number and ages of dependents.

6. *The Post 9/11 GI Bill (PGIB) Data* include several files that have been maintained by DMDC since September 2015 and contain detailed information from the VA on PGIB usage and transfer by individual service members. While there are plans to update the files monthly, we were able to obtain the September files only due to the timing of our project. These files contain individual-level data on the cumulative number of months and outlays by category of PGIB benefit used by each service member as of September 2015, and the institution(s) where the benefit was used. The data also include information on the dependent(s) to which the service member had transferred his/her benefit as of September 2015, and usage data by dependents where applicable.

7. *The Tuition Assistance Data (TA Data)* are maintained by each of the individual services and contain detailed records on number of credits earned, institution where those credits were delivered, and payments for eligible college expenses for all service members from fiscal year (FY) 2003 to FY 2015. DMDC col-

---

[1]   We do not include information on service members in the Coast Guard. We do include information on service members in the active component, and in the reserve components (the Guard and the Reserves).

lected the TA Data from each of the services and transferred it to RAND for the purposes of our project.

We linked these databases at the individual level across time using a scrambled identifier provided to us by DMDC to create a longitudinal database, tracking cohorts of new military service members from 2001 or the time of entry (whichever came last) to 2014 or exit (whichever came first). The file includes detailed individual-level information captured when the service member accessed (including demographic information, education, dependents, and AFQT scores); time-varying information on promotion and pay (including detailed information on education-related pay) while in the service; information on the timing of separation from service and transitions from the active to the reserve component (and vice versa); detailed information on TA usage while in the service; and detailed information on the cumulative incidence, as of September 2015, of PGIB usage, transfer, and usage by dependents both during and post-service. (Appendix C.1 includes a table of summary statistics).

Descriptive Analysis of PGIB and TA Usage

In this subsection, we describe patterns in PGIB and TA usage over time and across services. For PGIB, we show patterns in usage and transfer and break out overall costs by different categories. For TA, we describe patterns in usage, costs, and types of courses taken by service members using TA. We also show that the cost per semester of credit is significantly higher for PGIB than for TA, and this is primarily due to the living stipend that accompanies PGIB benefits.

As of September 2015, when DMDC first began regularly collecting the PGIB data, more than 1.2 million service members had used the PGIB, at a total cost of over $39 billion.[2] The transfer file we received indicates that over 450,000 service members had transferred at least some portion of their PGIB benefit as of late 2015. Transfers to spouses are not uncommon, but most who transfer the benefit transfer at least a portion to one or more children. Service members who transferred the benefit transferred, on average, about 29 of the (possible) 36 months.[3]

It is not clear how best to assess the take-up rate of the PGIB. Over the time period included in our data, 140,000 to 175,000 non–prior service enlisted personnel

---

[2] PGIB spending is reported in nominal dollars, not adjusted for inflation, because the PGIB files do not indicate the date of each payment.

[3] Recall that some service members are eligible for less than 36 months of benefits. This suggests that the vast majority who transfer, transfer most or all benefits. Also, service members who have transferred the benefit to multiple dependents can shift the number of months between themselves and the dependents. These data indicate that many service members have transferred the benefit in a manner that provides considerable flexibility in how they eventually use the benefit.

enter the military per year, along with some 15,000 to 19,000 officers. The vast majority of these personnel serve long enough to qualify to use the PGIB themselves. While
the force size has varied somewhat, this suggests that about the same number of service members (perhaps 175,000) exit each year, and most are eligible to use the PGIB.
Based on this rough calculation, there are likely to be more than 2 million veterans
from the active component who qualify, suggesting a take-up rate on the order of 60
percent (~1.2 million users / ~2 million eligible).[4] This suggests that the take-up rate
among service members or veterans who qualify is relatively high (recall that some service members may have used the PGIB prior to leaving the military). The proportion
serving long enough to transfer is much lower, with roughly one-third serving beyond
six years. Of course, the existence of this benefit is likely to influence reenlistment, as
detailed later in the chapter. But based on this very rough estimate, it is not surprising
that about one-third as many service members have transferred as have used the PGIB
for themselves.

As of September 2015, at least some transferred benefits had been used by nearly
250,000 dependents (spouses or children of service members). Roughly 700,000 dependents have had some PGIB benefits transferred to them but have not yet begun to use
the benefits (recall that service members can transfer benefits to multiple dependents).
Spouses make up about 56 percent of dependents who have used the benefit. In contrast, the majority of dependents who have received transferred benefits but have *not*
yet begun to use them are children (children make up over 85 percent of this group).
This difference is not surprising; while young children who receive the benefit may be
years from college, spouses are of an age that they may start college more immediately.
However, this difference has implications for costs: Those who use the benefit while
their spouses remain in service are not eligible for the living allowance, while children
who use the benefit (while or after their parent remains in service) are eligible for the
living allowance. This is one reason costs of the PGIB are likely to increase in the
future.

The PGIB data include only the total spending across all years per service member
in most categories. Tuition and the monthly living allowance[5] are the predominant
categories, but the data also include spending on books, tutorial services, licenses, and
exams, as well as Yellow Ribbon funds and "kickers" associated with Chapters 30, 33,
or 1606.[6] Tuition and fees, the living allowance, spending through the Yellow Ribbon

---

[4]   This figure accords reasonably well with the 2.8 million estimate of the total number of post-9/11 veterans
provided by the VA (the VA figure also includes those who served only in the reserve components). See VA, 2016a.

[5]   The monthly living allowance was originally based on the BAH benefit received by an E-5 with dependents.
Like BAH, the living allowance varies based on the geographic location (of the school), but all recipients attend-
ing a school at a given location receive the same allowance. The housing allowance is expected to vary from the
BAH in the future.

[6]   We would like to express our appreciation to Scott Seggerman and Vincent Suich at DMDC for their assistance in providing and understanding the data.

Program, and books are the highest cost components of PGIB funds spent, and these total nearly all funds spent. Spending on the living allowance slightly exceeds spending on tuition and fees, spending on books makes up about 5 percent of the total, spending on Yellow Ribbon Program funds makes up about 2 percent of the total, and spending on all other categories combined makes up about 2 percent of total spending.[7] Figure 5.1 includes the average spending (as of 2015) in each category, separated by spending on service members, spending on spouses, and spending on children.

Note that the spending reported in Figure 5.1 is not normed by year or month; it represents simply the average amount spent at the time our data were collected. Average spending on children, to date, is higher than average spending on spouses. A driver of this difference is the restriction that spouses who use PGIB while the sponsoring service member remains in service are not eligible for the living allowance (because the service member already receives BAH). Children have also used more months of benefits, on average, than spouses or former service members; this, too, contributed to the differences in Figure 5.1. (Later, we calculate a rough measure of spending per semester to adjust for these differences).

Figure 5.1
PGIB Spending, by Category and Service Member or Dependents

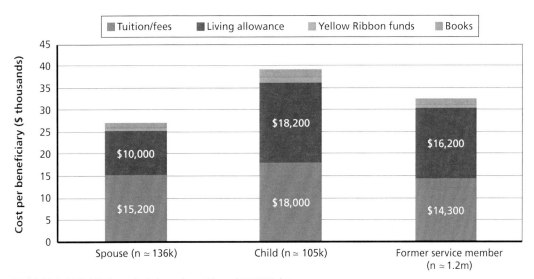

SOURCE: RAND NDRI analysis based on VA and DMDC data.
RAND RR1766-5.1

---

[7] The Yellow Ribbon Program is essentially a cost-sharing program between some higher education institutions and the VA. When schools with tuition rates above the PGIB maximum elect to take part in the program, the VA makes additional funds are available to service members and dependents who attend these schools; the schools generally agree to accept less than the full tuition payment. For program details, see VA, 2016b.

The transfer benefit is a unique aspect of the PGIB, and it is likely to influence service members from different eras in different ways. In particular, nearly all service members serving on 9/11, and nearly all who joined between 9/11 and the passage of the PGIB, became eligible for the benefit in 2009. Many of these personnel had already left the military; many others had already decided to remain for a full career. These decisions were unlikely to be affected by the PGIB. In contrast, service members serving in 2008, or who joined in 2008 or after, are much more likely to make decisions based in part on this benefit. Therefore, in later sections of this chapter, we examine continuation rates of those who were making decisions just prior to the bill's passage and compare their decisions with the decisions of service members after the bill was passed. Here, we provide some descriptive statistics on who has used the bill and who has transferred the bill to date. We divide the data based on era of enlistment.

Among former service members who have used the PGIB themselves, most were enlisted: About 6 percent served as officers, and about 1 percent served as warrant officers. About one-quarter entered the military prior to 2002; nearly 40 percent entered between 2002 and 2008. Thus, to date, more than 60 percent of service members who have used the PGIB entered the military before the bill passed. The typical service member who had used the benefit by September 2015 served a single term.

The PGIB files do not include the number of courses or credits completed. However, the files *do* include the current monthly living allowance payment, as well as the total living allowance payments to date—from this information it is, in some circumstances, possible to estimate the total number of months the service member has received benefits (although this calculation will be inaccurate in the cases of service members who move and/or transfer schools while receiving the bill, among other cases). Our data show that of the service members using the PGIB, about 25 percent have completed no more than seven months of school, while 25 percent have completed at least 20 months (on average, a service member had completed about 13 months of school). Spouses appear to have completed nearly 13 months on average, while children appear to have completed an average of 15 months.[8] As discussed above, our data do not include indications of exactly when those receiving benefits began doing so, or of the estimated months to complete a degree or program. Therefore, little can be gleaned about completion rates from these statistics; they indicate only that, on average, children have received a few more months of benefits than other users.

Based on the assumption that four months of PGIB benefits is equivalent to one semester of credit, and our rough estimate of months completed, those collecting PGIB had been enrolled in school for nearly 20 million months total as of September 2015; this suggests that students using PGIB earned something on the order of 5 million

---

[8]   This calculation is likely to be quite inaccurate for spouses, because spouses who use the benefit while their sponsor is still serving will not collect a living allowance. All of our semester-based calculations will be less accurate if those using the PGIB did not complete substantial numbers of classes; again, we have no information on class or program completion.

semesters of credit over this time period. Therefore, the (very roughly estimated) cost per semester is over $9,000 (including more than $4,000 in tuition). In Appendix B, we include a descriptive analysis of the institutions attended by service members using PGIB, as well as those using TA.

The TA file is a course-level (rather than an individual-level) file.[9] This file includes information on each course paid for with TA funds over the time period included in our data (FY 2003 to FY 2015). This includes information on about 9 million different courses. We are able to aggregate the data to understand the number of courses taken by each service member; we are also able to merge the data with our other files. TA covers tuition, up to a per–credit hour limit, with a maximum benefit limit of $4,500 per year (see Appendix A for more details on TA).

The TA file shows an overall decrease in the number of TA courses per year, from a maximum of more than 850,000 courses per year in 2004 to just under 500,000 in 2015. The decrease does not appear to be related to the passage of the PGIB; rather, it appears related to a drop in course-taking among Army personnel (see Figure 5.2).

About 1 million service members took at least one TA course over this period (FY 2003 to FY 2015). This suggests that a large minority of ser-

Figure 5.2
TA Courses per Year, by Service

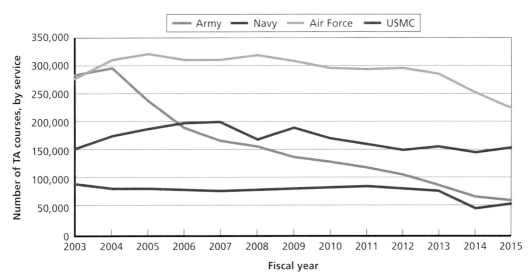

SOURCE: RAND NDRI analysis, based on TA data.

RAND *RR1766-5.2*

---

[9]   We would like to express our appreciation to the service representatives who provided these data; to Dawn Bilodeau and Jonathan Woods of DoD Voluntary Education, who approved and coordinated the provision of the data; and to Scott Seggerman of DMDC, who assisted with data transmittal.

vice members utilize TA.[10] The average cost per service member who uses TA is about $5,000; the average number of courses per service member is about nine.[11] Of course, our data are censored—we see only courses taken in FY 2003 or later, and some whom we observe will continue to take courses in the future. Service members who spend longer in the military have more time to take courses. On average, service members who take at least one TA course in our data set take roughly two courses per FY; about one-quarter of service members who use TA take 12 or more credits (typically, three or more courses) per year. A few service members take a very large number of courses (about 1 percent of service members using TA take 40 or more courses; this is roughly enough courses to complete a four-year degree).

A typical course listed in the TA data set lasts about 60 calendar days (this is substantially shorter than the traditional 15-week semester course). However, a typical course awards three hours of credit, suggesting the courses are frequently compressed. A typical service member attends a single institution, but attending two institutions is the norm among service members who take more than nine courses, and we see cases of service members attending three or more institutions. Most service members do not approach the yearly cost limit (11 of 12 in the data set spend under $4,500 per year). The majority of records indicate passing grades (although about 8 percent of records do not have a grade recorded). Figure 5.3 shows the distribution of grades in TA courses.

The TA data set lacks detailed information on the level of the course (no standard codes to indicate level of subject matter are included), but the data do include course titles. These vary dramatically in terms of the level of detail included. However, we were able to analyze the information by selecting the first 60 characters from each course title (examination of a subsample of the data suggested that the basic subject information generally was included in the first part of each title). We include some analyses of these data in Appendix B; the results indicate that service members frequently use TA to take a variety of introductory courses. We also include in Appendix B a short analysis of the institutions attended by service members using TA. While our data set includes information on courses taken at some 4,700 different institutions, institutions that educate large numbers of service members offered most courses. Indeed, only ten institutions offer 40 percent of courses. This suggests that these institutions specialize in providing courses to service members; for example, the compressed schedules noted above are likely to be a response to service members' preferences. While these schools are less selective than some, the limited data available on median earnings suggests that graduates of these schools have respectable long-term outcomes (Appendix B).

---

[10]   As of late 2015, there were about 3.7 million service members and veterans who had served in the post-9/11 era; this includes officers and enlisted personnel across components. It is mostly enlisted personnel in the active component who use TA; in any given year, there are about 1 million enlisted personnel in the active component and about 150,000 new enlisted personnel.

[11]   Due to the large number of courses taken by a few service members, the average of nine courses is skewed; the majority of TA users complete fewer than five courses.

Figure 5.3
Distribution of TA Course Grades

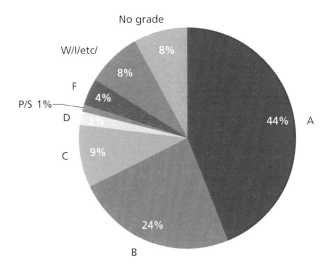

No grade

W/I/etc/

F

P/S 1%

D

C

8%

8%

4%

2%

9%

44%   A

24%

B

SOURCE: RAND NDRI analysis based on TA data.
NOTES: P/S = Pass or Satisfactory; F = Fail; "W/I/etc." indicates the
student withdrew or received an incomplete or similar grade. No
grade is recorded in about 8 percent of records.
RAND RR1766-5.3

In summary, our analyses indicate that many service members use TA to take introductory coursework. Such coursework could be viewed as a preparation for additional college in the future, but also could be viewed as a way to increase service members' human capital and productivity in the short run. Most service members accrue relatively few credits through TA. However, even small amounts of college credit have been shown to have a positive impact on civilian earnings (Kane and Rouse, 1995). While further research is needed to quantify the impact of small amounts of college on civilian earnings of veterans, these results suggest they are likely to be positive as well. We estimate that TA has been used to earn about 1.6 million semesters of college credit over the course of our data set (assuming 15 hours of credit is equivalent to one college semester, and excluding the courses for which there was not a passing grade assigned). The average cost per semester of TA is about $3,000.[12] Recall that our estimate of cost per semester of PGIB is about $9,000; thus, our calculations suggest that TA is much cheaper than PGIB on a per-semester credit basis (indeed, TA appears substantially

---

[12] This is a relatively conservative estimate, in which we calculate hours based on courses for which the service member received a passing grade. In other words, the average cost per course is about $500, but in some cases service members received failing grades, incomplete grades, or no grades; these courses are not considered to have provided hours of credit to the service member. If we instead assume that service members actually received credit for the courses that have no grade in our data, the estimated cost would fall about $200.

cheaper than the tuition costs of PGIB). However, PGIB has allowed service members and dependents to earn far more college credit than TA to date. This is not surprising, given the different designs of the two programs. Here, we note that over 300,000 service members used both TA and PGIB during the years included in our data sets. In a later section of this chapter, we analyze the extent to which TA and PGIB work together for service members.

Hypotheses

Here, we briefly summarize the primary hypotheses that we test empirically in this chapter. First, since the PGIB increased the generosity of educational benefits available to service members, we would expect that, all else equal, it would be easier for recruiters to attract high-quality service members. In our analysis, we tested two definitions of *high-quality* for enlisted personnel: (1) the commonly used definition: those with a high school or equivalent credential and an AFQT score placing them in the top half of high school graduates nationally, and (2) those with AFQT scores above the 65th percentile of the nation. The second definition is more stringent; it includes about one-quarter of enlistees, and these enlistees are likely to qualify for many of the more technical military occupations. The two definitions yielded similar results. Here we present the results for the first definition.

The hypotheses for the impact of PGIB passage on retention are more nuanced. First, because service members with PGIB benefits have relatively more attractive options in the civilian world than they did with MGIB, we would anticipate PGIB passage to result in lower retention rates, all else equal. However, because service members are able to transfer their PGIB benefits to their dependents after six years of service if they commit to an additional four years, we anticipate the likely negative impact of PGIB passage on retention rates for service members with dependents to be attenuated relative to those without dependents. While we have no *a priori* hypothesis about the *net* effect of PGIB passage on retention for service members with dependents, as we have no hypothesis about the relative magnitude of the decreased retention from PGIB overall and the increased relative retention for those with dependents, we expect the effect to be less negative than the effect for those without dependents.

Finally, we have no *a priori* hypotheses about the relationship between PGIB passage and TA usage. On the one hand, having access to the PGIB may induce service members to delay their education until separation from service, to take advantage of greater education benefits that include a living stipend. On the other hand, service members may elect to use more TA benefits to ensure that they are able to complete an academic credential during the 36 months of PGIB benefits or use them toward a graduate degree, or may wish to accumulate credits using TA to save some of their PGIB benefit to transfer to one or more dependents.

In addition to testing the above hypotheses, we also assess the relationship between education benefit usage and promotion tempo for enlisted personnel (enlisted personnel make up the vast majority of TA users). Here, we anticipate that the usage of education benefits is likely to be positively related to promotion tempo because TA and PGIB are both likely to attract more-productive service members, help them obtain valuable skills that aid in achieving promotion milestones, and, when accessed, serve as an indicator of quality to those making promotion decisions.

Summary of Quantitative Approaches

Evaluating our primary hypotheses presents various difficulties because of the specifics of PGIB and the time period during which the bill was passed and enacted (we discuss these challenges in Chapter One). Estimation of the effects of a program requires a counterfactual comparison group with which the trends after implementation can be contrasted. One common identification strategy is to use a difference-in-differences estimator, where the change in the outcome of interest over the same time period for an unaffected population is set against the change in outcome for the population affected. Unfortunately, there is no good comparable population to the U.S. military, even if we had measurements of the various outcomes for alternative populations. Therefore, comparisons will have to be within the military—across time, geography, or demographics. Because many of the benefits of PGIB were rolled out universally and identically across geographies, services, and components, we are limited in which hypotheses we can address using the difference-in-differences strategy. However, certain elements of the benefits or incentives faced do vary over populations within the military.

To empirically assess the primary hypotheses framed above, we will use five primary empirical strategies: (1) interrupted time-series at the national level, (2) difference-in-differences for strategic differential responses across service member attributes, (3) difference-in-differences and triple difference estimators for regional analyses where we leverage states that already had similar education programs in place, (4) within-person pre-post analysis (fixed effects) for repeated choices that service members make, and (5) when all else fails, by-person cross-sectional regressions of decisions, the least rigorous of our approaches.

All of our empirical approaches described below are some version of one of these five methodologies. The exact specifications, such as variables included, are detailed next. We discuss each individual hypothesis, grouped by the time in the service member's career.[13]

---

[13] We control for multiple hypotheses using Benjamini-Hochberg false discovery rates, with each family being defined by the hypotheses listed following. Also, note that we tested for, and found, evidence of parallel trends prior to the passage of the PGIB, across both service member attributes and regions; this suggests that the difference-in-differences strategies are appropriate.

1. Interrupted Time-Series

For certain outcomes, benefits were universally and identically rolled out, and so the best strategy is an interrupted time-series regression, controlling for as many relevant factors as we can. We will use as our example the impact of receiving PGIB benefits on continuation rates in the military. The new education bill allowed for all service members who honorably complete their first contract of service to be eligible to use PGIB education benefits for themselves whenever they like. All services and components received the new benefit structure and incentives at the same time: passed in June 2008 and in effect as of August 2009. Given the universal rollout, there is no comparison population to which we can contrast continuation rates. As an alternative, interrupted time-series regressions look for a structural break in the trend over time at a specific date, controlling for other observable factors. It assumes that any factors not directly controlled for in the regression are the PGIB estimated effect. If there are other structural shifts, contemporaneous policy changes, or changes in military engagements at the same time, we will be unable to separate out those effects. To address these as best we can, we include as many confounding factors for which we have data. Equation 7.1 describes the regressions.

$$Y_{isgt} = \beta_0 + \beta_1 PGIB_t + \beta_{t1}t + \beta_{t2}t^2 + X_{it}\beta_X + Z_{st}\beta_Z + W_{gt}\beta_G + \varepsilon_{isgt} \qquad (7.1)$$

Consider, for example, the outcome Y for whether the service member continues in the military past six years of service. Then the outcome for service member i in service and component s from state g in year t is a function of time-related factors (a quadratic in time given by t, as well as the potential structural change after passage of PGIB), service member characteristics (X), service and component characteristics (Z), and state characteristics (W). The time-related factors are the most important in the specification with regard to the identification. In essence, after controlling for all other factors in X, Z, and W, we allow for there to be a (potentially) quadratic time trend in continuation rates from 2001 to 2014, with a potential discontinuity for being after the passage of PGIB in the summer of 2008 ($PGIB_t$). That discontinuity (given by β_1), if it exists, represents the effect of the PGIB benefits on the continuation rate. The additional service member factors, service and component factors, and state trends help control for other factors that may be correlated with the timing of PGIB, as well as yield additional precision to the estimates for more efficient hypothesis testing. The specific factors are described in detail with relation to each individual test to follow. For some regressions, such as the entry quality, we collapse the data to year/month/state/service entry cohorts and their average quality. The regression remains otherwise the same.

2. Difference-in-Differences Across Service Member Characteristics

There are certain hypotheses for which we can use differential impacts on subpopulations to do a difference-in-differences analysis. We use as our example here the impact of the transferability criterion of PGIB. We assume that service members who have dependents are more likely to be affected by the transferability criterion than service members with no current dependents.[14]

Instead of relying only on the change from before and after passage of PGIB, as in the interrupted time-series regressions unable to separate out contemporaneous changes, we can now use service members without dependents as a control. They would plausibly be affected by all the same other unobserved or contemporaneous factors as those with dependents, so that we can use them as a counterfactual for what the change in the outcome would be for those with dependents over the same time period. This is described by Equation 7.2.

$$Y_{isgt} = \beta_0 + \beta_1 PGIB_t + \beta_2 D_{it} + \beta_3 PGIB_t \times D_{it} + \beta_{t1} t +$$
$$\beta_{t2} t^2 + X_{it}\beta_X + Z_{st}\beta_Z + W_{gt}\beta_G + \varepsilon_{isgt} \qquad (7.2)$$

The variables are the same as in the interrupted time-series description above, with the addition of an indicator for a demographic characteristic across which incentives differ (in our example, having dependents), given by D. The parameter of interest, given the difference-in-differences specification, is now given by β_3. The indexes and other variable names follow the same as described above in the description of the interrupted time-series.

3. Difference-in-Differences and Triple Differences Across Affected States

We do additional analysis looking at three states that had similar education benefits prior to passage of PGIB. This allows for a comparison of the service member outcomes in the states that already had similar benefits with the trends of service members in states in the same census region. This frames a difference-in-differences analysis. We can do a triple difference analysis by additionally looking across service member characteristics, such as if they have dependents, as described above. The three states we investigate are Wisconsin, Texas, and Illinois.

For Wisconsin (WI), we look at the Wisconsin GI Bill (WGIB), passed in 2005. The Wisconsin GI bill allowed all service members, as well as any dependents, to receive a free education at any Wisconsin public institute of higher education. This program is in ways more generous than PGIB in allowing the service member *and* his or her dependents to fully use the benefits but has lower value in the sense of limiting college choices to Wisconsin public schools. It allows us to investigate the outcomes

---

[14] While service members who do not currently have dependents might expect to in the future, this would bias our estimate toward zero, so any statistically significant effect we find yields insight into the hypothesis.

for WI service members before and after the 2005 passage of WGIB compared with those in neighboring states that had no change in education benefits over that period, as well as to contrast WI service members, who had little to no change in education benefits with PGIB passing (because of WGIB), in contrast with neighboring state service members, who saw an increase.

For Texas (TX), we look at the Hazelwood Act, passed in 1923. Hazelwood allows all service members who enter the service in Texas and complete at least 181 days of active service to receive up to 150 credit hours of education tuition-free at any public institution of higher education in TX to which they are accepted. With the passing of the Legacy Program in 2009, children may also use any unused portion of the benefits if they are under age 25 and are Texas residents. This makes the bill difficult to contrast with PGIB. Hazelwood can be both a substitute and a complement to PGIB. When PGIB passed in 2008, those without dependents were similarly affected in TX and surrounding states, with TX service members perhaps reacting less strongly to the expanded benefits than neighboring service members because of their preexisting benefits (although both PGIB and Hazelwood can be used). We would expect TX service members with dependents to have larger decreases in retention than non-Texan service members with dependents because of the Legacy Program, such that they do not need to reach six-plus-four years of service to transfer education benefits.

For Illinois (IL), we use the Illinois Veteran Grant (IVG). Passed in 1967, IVG offers up to 120 credit hours in public higher education institutes in Illinois for Illinois-resident service members with at least a year of completed active duty. There is no transferability of the education benefits to dependents; however, IL service members can, for example, use IVG for themselves and transfer PGIB to their dependents (conditional on meeting the PGIB requirements). We hypothesize that IL service members will have a smaller decrease in continuation rates after PGIB because of their existing IVG benefits. In essence, they see a smaller increase in overall benefits because of redundancies between the two programs than non-IL service members, who gain from migrating the MGIB to the PGIB. For those with dependents, we expect, if anything, a small positive difference for Illinois service members over non-Illinois service members (compared with the same change for those without dependents), because of the preexisting benefits they had.

4. Fixed Effects Pre-Post Regression

In certain cases, we observe service members' decisions repeated times. Consider, for example, the decision to use tuition assistance in a given six-month span (the frequency of the data). We can do a within-person fixed effects regression that allows us to investigate how a person's decisions changed before and after passage of PGIB. Equation 7.3 outlines the regression we perform. It is similar to equation 7.1 for the interrupted time-series regression, except now we include an individual fixed effect ψ_i that improves identification by looking at *changes* in service member behavior.

$$Y_{isgt} = \beta_0 + \beta_1 PGIB_t + \beta_{t1}t + \beta_{t2}t^2 + X_{it}\beta_X + Z_{st}\beta_Z + W_{gt}\beta_G + \psi_i + \varepsilon_{isgt} \qquad (7.3)$$

5. By-Person Regressions

At times, we will want to understand the relationship between behaviors. We can do this only by conducting simple by-person regressions. This is described by Equation 7.4, where A is the variable for which we want to identify the impact on the outcome Y. For example, to look at how TA use affects promotion tempo, we will have only one observation per service member, so we cannot use a fixed effects estimator, and we are not looking at a policy change. We are capturing only the correlation between the two, and not the effect of taking more TA on promotion. As such, it captures the signal impact (signaling to superiors their quality), the impact of additional human capital from the TA, and the selection effect (service members likely to take TA in the first three years of service may be of higher quality on various dimensions that also affect promotion tempo). We describe the competing correlations in these situations.

$$Y_{isgt} = \beta_0 + \beta_1 A_{it} + \beta_{t1}t + \beta_{t2}t^2 + X_{it}\beta_X + Z_{st}\beta_Z + W_{gt}\beta_G + \varepsilon_{isgt} \qquad (7.4)$$

Impact of PGIB Passage on Recruitment

Table 5.1 presents the recruitment hypothesis we investigate, as well as the theoretical evidence and empirical approaches. For this report, we investigate only one hypothesis about recruitment, namely that the increased education benefits would attract more academically qualified enlistees, resulting in higher average academic quality of entering cohorts.

Recruitment Hypothesis: Increased Quality of Enlistees

We hypothesize that the increase of education benefits offered by PGIB should increase the academic quality of new enlistees. We measure academic quality as the average AFQT score, the proportion of *high quality* (AFQT at or above 50 and a high school diploma), the proportion of enlistees with some college, and the proportion with an undergraduate degree. For comparison, we also include the overall size of the entry

Table 5.1
Entry Hypotheses, Theoretical Evidence, and Empirical Approaches

Hypothesis	Theoretical Evidence	Empirical Approach 1	Empirical Approach 2
1. Higher benefits increase quality of enlistees.	Theory says yes, focus groups are less aware of PGIB as motivator.	National level ITS OLS regressions of enlistment quality measures on PGIB	Wisconsin WGIB & PGIB DID regressions of enlistment quality measures

cohorts (independent of quality). We look at both the counts of high quality and the fraction of each entering cohort that is high quality.

Theory predicts an increase in academic quality of new cohorts, as the marginal recruit who is high quality and interested in education after service would be more likely to join. However, our focus groups with service members suggested that the structure of the education benefits was not an important factor in their recruitment decision. The service members knew that GI benefits existed but didn't know what those benefits were, and may not have processed changes in the education benefits brought on by the change from MGIB to PGIB. We take two approaches to address this hypothesis empirically.

The first approach uses the interrupted time-series regression, collapsed to year/month/state/service entry cohorts. We regress the quality outcomes on a variable indicating that the recruited cohort occurred after the passage of the PGIB. We also include the following individual indicators, aggregated: the fraction of the cohort that is each race and the fraction female. We include state dummy variables as well as the unemployment rate in the month and state of interest. We include the authorized strength of the service and service dummies, as well as the quadratic in the date. Table 5.2 reports the coefficient on PGIB, the potential discontinuity after passage of PGIB. We find somewhat mixed results for the counts, but this is the effect of change in both quality and size of the cohorts. The averages are uniformly positive for both the active and reserve components, although the effect sizes are two or more times larger for reservists. The effects are significant and, although not very large, are still of a size that is meaningful. For example, about 70 percent of the enlistees on average are of high qual-

Table 5.2
Enlistment Quality Hypothesis 1 Regression Results: Change in Cohort Quality Post-PGIB (all services), Monthly Enlistment Cohorts (coefficient on post-PGIB reported)

	Component	Count	Mean AFQT	Proportion High AFQT	Some College	Undergrad
Count	Active	14.11	—	0.915	−3.111***	1.285**
		(6.888)	—	(4.568)	(0.876)	(0.414)
	Reserves	−0.987	—	2.512***	0.881***	1.199***
		(1.078)	—	(0.511)	(0.177)	(0.0915)
Mean	Active	-	0.637**	0.00459	0.00934	0.0155***
		-	(0.182)	(0.00440)	(0.00362)	(0.00201)
	Reserves	-	2.386***	0.0847***	0.0366***	0.0330***
		-	(0.285)	(0.00757)	(0.00466)	(0.00266)

NOTES: ***$p < 0.01$, **$p < 0.05$, *$p < 0.1$, adjusted for multiple hypotheses.

Standard errors in parentheses. Control variables: state unemployment rate, service authorized strength, quadratic in year, fraction each race, fraction female, state dummies.

ity. A 1.5– to 3.5–percentage point increase is not negligible. Table C.1 in the appendix reports selected regression results by service; the Army appears to have benefited most from increased enlistment cohort quality after passage of PGIB.

Next, we look at the same regressions for Wisconsin and the states in its census region. We can look both at Wisconsin after passage of WGIB and Wisconsin and the other states after PGIB. Table 5.3 presents the results. The Wisconsin trends do not confirm the hypothesis of increased quality from better education benefits. It is unclear whether this is representative of the true effect of PGIB from the better identification strategy, or that either Wisconsin or WGIB are not representative of PGIB. It could be that the national results are picking up a contemporaneous trend of smaller but higher-quality cohorts that spiked around that time, and the national results are not indicative of the effect of PGIB. On the other hand, WGIB might have received less notice and announcement than PGIB (or more), or recruiting officers may not have been given instructions to emphasize it.

Across both of these empirical methodologies, we find mixed to modestly positive results for the impact of PGIB on enlistee quality. In one case, we find positive and statistically significant indications of changes in enlistee average academic quality after PGIB, while in the other we find no and insignificant changes. The positive results, due to an interrupted time-series approach, may as noted be indicative of other changes going on around the same time, and not due to PGIB—or they may be the results of PGIB. Based on all the evidence, our preferred estimate is at most a 1–percentage point increase in quality (either proportion high quality or proportion exceeding an AFQT

Table 5.3
Enlistment Quality Hypothesis 1 Wisconsin Regression Result: Change in Cohort Quality Post-PGIB (all services), Monthly Enlistment Cohorts (coefficient on post-PGIB reported)

Component	Quality Measure	WGIB x WI	PGIB x WI
Active	Mean AFQT	0.00543	0.581
		(0.575)	(0.399)
	Prop. High AFQT 1	−2.4005	0.0168
		(0.0129)	(0.0100)
Reserves	Mean AFQT	−1.674	1.082
		(0.955)	(0.683)
	Prop. High AFQT 1	−0.0422	0.0407
		(0.0248)	(0.0178)
Hypothesized direction		+	−

NOTES: ***$p < 0.01$, **$p < 0.05$, *$p < 0.1$, adjusted for multiple hypotheses.

Standard errors in parentheses. Control variables: state unemployment rate, service authorized strength, quadratic in year, fraction each race, fraction female, state dummies score of 65) after the passage of the PGIB. Therefore, we conclude that there is, at most, evidence of a small increase in recruit quality as a result of the PGIB's increased benefits, which aligns with our focus group experiences that suggest that service members know that there are education benefits, but not details (and thus changes in details), and are motivated to enlist mainly for other reasons.

Retention Outcomes

We next look at retention outcomes of service members. Table 5.4 presents the hypotheses we investigate, as well as the theoretical evidence and empirical approaches. We investigate two hypotheses of how education benefits affect retention. First, we investigate the overall effect of PGIB on retention. Second, we look at the differential effects of PGIB on retention for those with dependents.

We focus on retention at the end of the first term across various horizons. Defining first-term retention across the services and over time is not straightforward; first terms vary in length, and some service members choose at the end of their first term to extend their careers for relatively short periods of time rather than reenlisting (or departing). Also, there was some use of "stop loss" during the period covered by our data. Finally, reenlistment was not recorded in the same manner by different services in the files provided by DMDC. For all of these reasons, we estimate models of continuation rather than reenlistment per se. Although many service members remain in the military for an entire career, the end of the first term is the most common time frame to leave the military. Figure 5.4 graphs the unconditional retention by years of service; the drop at the end of the first term is evident. For service members who remain past roughly 12 years, continuing to at least 20 years of service is extremely common. Thus, by focusing on the end of the first term, we are focusing on a period of time that encompasses a key decision. At the end of the first term, all service members are eligible for the PGIB; however, to be able to transfer the benefit, service members must reenlist.

Table 5.4
Retention Hypotheses, Theoretical Evidence, and Empirical Approaches

Hypothesis	Theoretical Evidence	Empirical Approach 1	Empirical Approach 2
1. Continuation rates drop from PGIB.	Increased benefits make them more likely to separate and get education.	National ITS Regressions on continuation on PGIB and controls	DD for Wisconsin, Texas, Illinois
2. The continuation drop is less for those with dependents.	The transfer eligibility requirement makes them more likely to extend.	DD national regressions of continuation on PGIB, dependents, interaction, and controls	DDD for Wisconsin

Figure 5.4
Probability of Remaining in Service, by Years of Prior Service

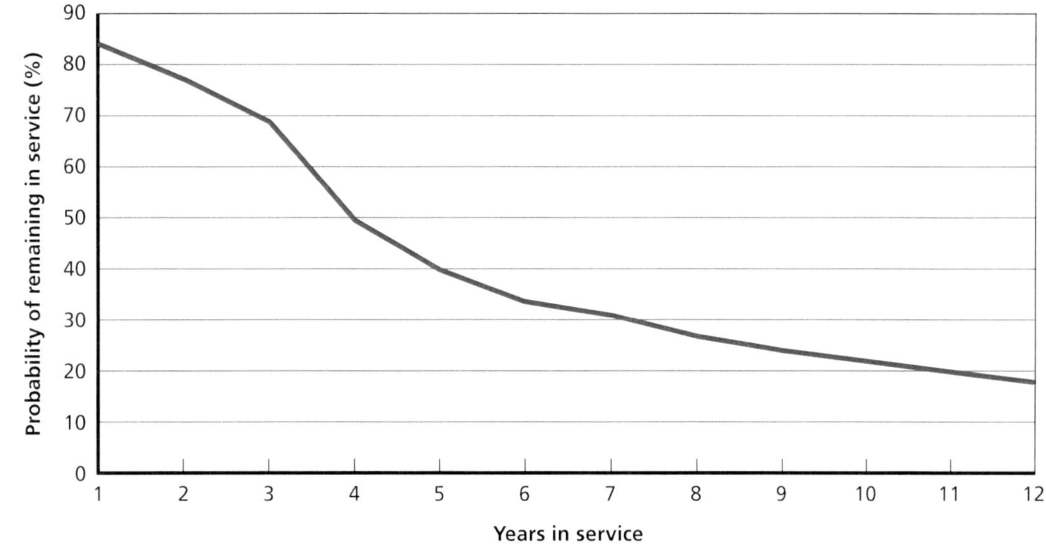

RAND *RR1766-5.4*

Retention Hypothesis 1: Overall, the Increased Benefits of PGIB Lead to a Decrease in Continuation Rates

We first evaluate how service members respond to the increased educational benefits of PGIB in terms of their continuation rates. We look at service members at 2.5 to four years of service and evaluate whether they continue in the military past five, past six, and past seven years of service. We hypothesize that, all else equal, the increased educational benefits improve their outside options and, thus, would decrease their continuation rates.

Our first empirical approach is the national interrupted time-series. We include as individual controls whether they have dependents, gender, race, whether they are high AFQT, service entry schooling experience, number of completed TA courses, age, number of months deployed in the last six months, skill level, pay/rank, and occupation. We include as service controls the authorized strength and indicators for which service the service member is in. We include as geographic controls an indicator for state of residence and the unemployment rate in that state. For time, we include a quadratic in the date and an indicator for the month of the survey to control for seasonality. The coefficient of interest is on the variable indicating that the observation was made after the passage of the PGIB. We estimate it separately for active and reserve components but allow for continuation to be in either component.

Table 5.5 presents the results for the national interrupted time-series coefficient on post-PGIB. For active, we find very consistent effects of a decrease in continuation rates of about 1 to 3 percentage points. Given that the average continuation rates at

Table 5.5
Retention Hypothesis 1, National Interrupted Time-Series Regression Results: Change in Continuation Rates Post-PGIB (all services), Coefficient on Post-PGIB Reported

Component	Service	Past 5	Past 6	Past 7
Active	Army	−0.0348***	−0.0284***	−0.0280***
		(0.00262)	(0.00290)	(0.00315)
	Navy	−0.0125***	−0.0264***	−0.0244***
		(0.00348)	(0.00381)	(0.00408)
	Marines	−0.0254***	−0.0232***	−0.0290***
		(0.00375)	(0.00380)	(0.00401)
	Air Force	−0.0116***	−0.0212***	−0.0187***
		(0.00337)	(0.00405)	(0.00441)
	All	−0.0241***	-0.0261***	−0.0275***
		(0.00160)	(0.00176)	(0.00190)
Reserves	Army	−0.00876***	−0.0259***	−0.0145***
		(0.00238)	(0.00329)	(0.00365)
	Navy	−0.0582***	−0.0545***	−0.0260
		(0.0137)	(0.0153)	(0.0163)
	Marines	0.0148	0.000274	−0.0127
		(0.00640)	(0.00902)	(0.00892)
	Air Force	0.0650***	0.0331	0.0254
		(0.0176)	(0.0235)	(0.0269)
	All	−0.00846***	−0.0261***	−0.0170***
		(0.00220)	(0.00300)	(0.00328)

Component	Past 5	Past 6	Past 7
Active	−0.0241***	−0.0261***	−0.0275***
	(0.00160)	(0.00176)	(0.00190)
Reserves	−0.00846***	−0.0261***	−0.0170***
	(0.00220)	(0.00300)	(0.00328)

NOTES: ***$p < 0.01$, **$p < 0.05$, *$p < 0.1$, adjusted for multiple hypotheses. Standard errors in parentheses. Control variables: having dependents, gender, race dummies, cumulative completed courses, high AFQT score, college attainment, age, months deployed in past six months, resident state unemployment rate, service authorized strength, quadratic in years, skill level, month dummies, state dummies, pay status dummies, military occupational specialty dummies, service dummies.

this point are around 75 percent, these effect sizes are of a reasonable size. The drop is largest for shorter horizons (past five years), and even more so proportionally, given that the average continuation rates are larger for longer horizons. Service members in the reserves have slightly smaller responses. Table C.2 in Appendix C reports the trends by service; the results are similar across services.

We look at additional empirical approaches that use a difference-in-differences approach that leverages already existing education benefit programs in certain states. The results of this are reported in Table 5.6. The first test looks at Wisconsin and WGIB. We have three separate coefficients that relate to this hypothesis. The first is the coefficient on the interaction between post-WGIB and service members being Wisconsin residents. Given the increased benefits that improve outside options, we would expect decreases in continuation rates. As shown in Table 5.6, this is what we find, and of the same magnitude as the national results. The results are not statistically significant (they are significant at the 10-percent level without adjustments for multiple hypotheses). Second, we can look at how non-Wisconsin service members from states near Wisconsin respond to PGIB. This is not a difference-in-differences estimate but shows the regional response to PGIB as an interrupted time-series. It is similar to the national results. Finally, we examine how Wisconsin service members respond relative to non-Wisconsin service members after passage of PGIB. We expect this coefficient to be positive if it is lined up with our hypothesis. And that is indeed what we find,

Table 5.6
Retention Hypothesis 1: Difference-in-Differences Regression Results: Change in Continuation Rates Post-PGIB, State Sub-Studies (all services)

Continuation Horizon	Wisconsin			Texas		Illinois	
	WGIB x WI	PGIB	PGIB x WI	PGIB	PGIB x TX	PGIB	PGIB x IL
Past 5	−0.0190	−0.0209***	0.0282***	−0.0166***	−0.0169***	−0.0251***	0.0147***
	(0.00945)	(0.00442)	(0.00605)	(0.00298)	(0.00285)	(0.00407)	(0.00430)
Past 6	−0.0137	−0.0173***	0.0172	−0.0230***	−0.0138***	−0.0225***	0.00546
	(0.00997)	(0.00479)	(0.00691)	(0.00328)	(0.00391)	(0.00445)	(0.00568)
Past 7	−0.0130	−0.0186***	0.0125	−0.0335***	−0.0143***	−0.0218***	0.0123
	(0.0101)	(0.00507)	(0.00797)	(0.00358)	(0.00333)	(0.00472)	(0.00493)
Hypothesized direction	−	−	+	−	+	−	+

NOTES: ***$p < 0.01$, **$p < 0.05$, *$p < 0.1$, adjusted for multiple hypotheses.

Standard errors in parentheses. Control variables: having dependents, gender, race dummies, cumulative completed courses, high AFQT score, college attainment, age, months deployed in past six months, resident state unemployment rate, service authorized strength, quadratic in years, skill level, month dummies, state dummies, pay status dummies, military occupational specialty dummies, service dummies.

essentially yielding a zero effect for the PGIB + PGIB × WI combination that is the total effect of Wisconsin service members. These are all consistent with our hypothesis.

Next, we take the case of Texas with Hazelwood. As discussed earlier, this case is not as clean cut, because PGIB still extended benefits of the service members beyond Hazelwood more strongly than WGIB.

Table 5.6 reports the primary results. We again report the regional interrupted time-series coefficients for passage of PGIB, which are consistent, negative and significant. We then look at how Texas service members responded differentially to the bill as compared to service members from states in the same census region. We expect these coefficients to be positive, as the difference in their benefits from pre-PGIB to post-PGIB is smaller than that for their neighbors. However, we find negative coefficients that are relatively large, almost doubling the non-TX coefficients. It is unclear why this is the case.

Finally, we look at the case of Illinois. The interrupted time-series PGIB effect is still negative. The differential effect of those in Illinois is, as expected, positive, reflecting the fact that Illinois service members already had similar benefits, and even though both benefits can be used, there is a decreasing advantage to doing so, so the increase in the outside option of leaving the military to go to school is not as strong.

Retention Hypothesis 2: The Increased Benefits of PGIB Have a Less Negative Effect for Those with Dependents Because of the Transfer Requirement

One generous aspect of PGIB is the provision that allows for transfer of the education benefits to dependents of the service members. To qualify, service members must have completed either ten years of service or six years of service with a commitment to serving four more years. Presumably, there are some service members on the margin between staying past six years or not who, with this additional incentive, may choose to extend.

Our first empirical approach is for the national level, a difference-in-differences that contrasts those with dependents and those with no dependents, before and after PGIB. The control variables are the same as in retention hypothesis 1 national interrupted time-series, described earlier. Table 5.7 presents the regression coefficients of interest from the difference-in-differences. We find those with dependents are less reactive to the PGIB decrease in continuation rates, presumably because of the transfer eligibility criteria. It approximately cuts the drop in continuation rates of those with no dependents in half. The effect is slightly stronger for shorter horizons, unlike the overall drop. Table C.4 in Appendix C reports the coefficients for by-service regressions. The Army has the largest response in most cases.

We also use the Wisconsin, Texas, and Illinois sub-studies to evaluate the same question using a triple difference strategy. Wisconsin and Texas do not require extension to qualify for transferability. Illinois does not allow for transfer of benefits to children. This allows for two tests: The interaction of PGIB with dependents exam-

Table 5.7
Retention Hypothesis 2, Difference-in-Differences Regression Results: Differential Change in Continuation Rates Post-PGIB for Those with Dependents (all services)

Component	Past 5	Past 6	Past 7
Active	0.0164***	0.0158***	0.0118***
	(0.00105)	(0.00122)	(0.00142)
Reserve	0.0139***	0.0241***	0.0197***
	(0.00156)	(0.00224)	(0.00262)

NOTES: ***$p < 0.01$, **$p < 0.05$, *$p < 0.1$, adjusted for multiple hypotheses.

Standard errors in parentheses. Control variables: having dependents, gender, race dummies, cumulative completed courses, high AFQT score, college attainment, age, months deployed in past six months, resident state unemployment rate, service authorized strength, quadratic in years, skill level, month dummies, state dummies, pay status dummies, military occupation specialty dummies, service dummies.

ines how those in neighboring states responded (similar to the national difference-in-differences), and the triple interaction between PGIB, the treated state, and having dependents examines if service members from the treated state who had dependents had a difference in the response (relative to those with dependents) than those from neighboring states with dependents. We hypothesize that, for Wisconsin and Texas, the triple difference should be negative, as service members have less need for the extension to get to six-plus-four years and PGIB extension ability, as they can use the PGIB for their own education and transfer the state benefits to their dependents. For Illinois, we expect, on the other hand, a positive and small (if any) effect that is reflective of their marginal benefit increase being smaller due to decreasing marginal returns to education and their higher education benefits, as well as redundancies between the two programs.

Table 5.8 presents the regression coefficients. For Wisconsin, the effects are all in the hypothesized direction, and the magnitude is reasonable. We find about 1– to 3–percentage point differences for those with dependents and those without when presented with additional benefits for transferability. For Texas, we find consistent results for PGIB passage (for neighboring states), and no difference for Texas service members after PGIB who have dependents. For Illinois, the surrounding states responded in similar ways, but there are mixed and statistically insignificant results for the state programs.

Relationship Between TA and PGIB Usage

Table 5.9 presents the benefit usage hypotheses we investigate, as well as the theoretical evidence and empirical approaches. We investigate four hypotheses of how education benefits affect in-service careers. First, we investigate the effect of PGIB on TA usage.

Table 5.8
Retention Hypothesis 2, Triple Difference Regression Results: Differential Change in
Continuation Rates Post-PGIB for Those with Dependents, State Sub-Studies (all services)

Continuation Horizon	Wisconsin		Texas		Illinois	
	PGIB x Dep.	PGIB x Dep. x WI	PGIB x Dep.	PGIB x Dep. x TX	PGIB x Dep.	PGIB x Dep. x IL
Past 5	0.0218***	−0.0253	0.0140***	0.00253	0.0258***	−0.00568
	(0.00287)	(0.00932)	(0.00189)	(0.00375)	(0.00270)	(0.00621)
Past 6	0.0160***	−0.0268	0.0128***	−0.000127	0.0213***	0.00860
	(0.00326)	(0.0106)	(0.00221)	(0.00434)	(0.00310)	(0.00714)
Past 7	0.00955	−0.0145	0.00946***	0.00629	0.0144***	0.00848
	(0.00373)	(0.0121)	(0.00258)	(0.00504)	(0.00358)	(0.00827)
Hypothesized Direction	+	−	+	−	+	+

NOTES: ***$p < 0.01$, **$p < 0.05$, *$p < 0.1$, adjusted for multiple hypotheses.

Standard errors in parentheses. Control variables: having dependents, gender, race dummies, cumulative completed courses, high AFQT score, college attainment, age, months deployed in past six months, resident state unemployment rate, service authorized strength, quadratic in years, skill level, month dummies, state dummies, pay status dummies, military occupational specialty dummies, service dummies.

Second, we look at the differential effects of PGIB on TA usage for those with dependents. We then look at the effects of TA and PGIB usage on promotion (third). Finally, we hypothesize that TA usage has an ambiguous effect on PGIB take-up.

Benefit Usage Hypothesis 1: Ambiguous Effects of PGIB on TA Usage

Our first hypothesis around in-service outcomes relating to education benefits is that the passage of PGIB had ambiguous effects on TA usage by service members. On one hand, PGIB is a substitute for TA, so that service members may opt for less TA usage (especially if educational credits are more difficult to achieve through TA when active service members are busy). On the other hand, TA may be considered a complement to PGIB if the service members want to pursue additional degrees or do both at a slower pace, or to transfer benefits to their dependents. Additionally, if the academic quality of enlistees really did increase after and as a result of PGIB, then the compositional changes from PGIB would also lead to an increase of TA usage.

Our first approach to addressing this question is the interrupted time-series approach. We regress the number of TA courses completed in each six-month period on whether it is after PGIB, the cumulative number of courses that service members had completed, their years of service, a quadratic in the year, and the following additional controls: whether they had dependents, whether they are high AFQT scorers, whether they entered the service with some college or an undergraduate degree, their

Table 5.9
Relationship Between TA and PGIB Usage, Theoretical Evidence, and Empirical Approaches

Hypothesis	Theoretical Evidence	Empirical Approach 1	Empirical Approach 2
1. Effect of PGIB on TA usage is ambiguous.	PGIB is a substitute, so may decrease, but PGIB and TA usage are correlated through service member quality, so may be positive.	Regress number of TA courses on PGIB passage, cumulative number of courses, years of service, years quadratic, lots of controls.	Fixed effect of approach 1
2. Effect of PGIB on TA usage is more positive for those with dependents.	PGIB is less of a substitute for those with dependents, who may want to use TA for themselves and PGIB for dependents. As such, the positive correlational effect may dominate more.	Regress number of TA courses on PGIB passage, PGIB interacted with dependents, cumulative number of courses, YOS, years quadratic, lots of controls.	Fixed effect of approach 1
3. The effect of TA and PGIB usage on promotion is ambiguous but should be more positive for TA than PGIB.	Higher-quality service members are both more likely to use TA and to be promoted or signal quality, but they may also be more likely to leave. Same for PGIB. TA is visible when up for promotion, unlike PGIB, and may be more difficult to take than PGIB, so more correlated with unobserved quality. Both of those things should make the coefficient on TA more positive.	Conditional on being in the service at the time, regress promotion status on TA usage (one observation per service member, #courses at the point where we mark 36m/48m/6y). For PGIB, conditional on being in the service at the time, regress promotion status on TA usage, PGIB usage, and interaction (one observation per service member, #courses at the point where we mark 36m/48m/6y, and conditional on us observing them at least two years after service).	
4. TA usage has ambiguous effect on PGIB use.	May be positive because of unobserved ability correlation, may be negative because they already have college credit	Regress PGIB uptake on TA usage + controls.	

race, their sex, their age, how many months in the period they were deployed, the unemployment rate in their state during that time, the authorized strength of their service that year, their skill level, dummies for what month it is, their state, their pay grade/rank, and their military occupational specialty (MOS)/occupation. For all service regressions, indicators for their service are also included.

We additionally evaluate the hypothesis using the fixed effects interrupted time-series regression approach. All time-varying covariates listed in the previous paragraph are also included. The fixed effects estimator allows us to control for underlying quality, separating out the complement of PGIB and TA usage from the change in cohort quality effect.

Table 5.10 presents the coefficients on PGIB in the regressions, the interrupted time-series estimator. For those serving in the active component, we find a clear and positive effect, suggesting that the complementary nature of TA and PGIB dominates

Table 5.10
In-Service Hypothesis 1, National Interrupted Time-Series Regressions, Change in TA Usage from Passage of PGIB (all services)

	Active	Reserve
Cross-Sectional	0.0974***	−0.0794
	(0.00930)	(0.0504)
Fixed Effects	0.146***	0.0355
	(0.0113)	(0.0662)

NOTES: ***$p < 0.01$, **$p < 0.05$, *$p < 0.1$, adjusted for multiple hypotheses.

Standard errors in parentheses. Control variables: total previously completed TA courses, years of service, having dependents, gender, race dummies, cumulative completed courses, high AFQT score, college attainment, age, months deployed in past six months, resident state unemployment rate, service authorized strength, quadratic in years, skill level, month dummies, state dummies, pay status dummies, MOS dummies, service dummies.

the substitution effect. The effects are not very small, with the coefficient around 0.1 additional TA courses each six months. Interestingly, the fixed effects estimators are larger for those in the active component. This suggests, among other things, that there is no strong increase in quality of new cohorts after PGIB that leads also to higher TA usage, else we would have observed a smaller fixed effect estimator. Regardless, the fixed effect estimator gives us confidence that service members actually increased TA usage after PGIB, and that it isn't cohort and compositional effects.

The effects for those serving in the reserve components are smaller and less significant. This may be partially a factor of TA usage being much lower among reservists than active component service members. This trend is demonstrated in Tables C.5 and C.6 in Appendix C; Table C.5 reports the coefficients by service. The same trends hold, and the Navy has the largest coefficients.

We will return to the question of substitute vs. complement when we look at the postservice hypotheses and contrast PGIB take-up for those with more or less TA.

We also look at the coefficient on the cumulative number of courses that the service members have taken. Table 5.11 shows the coefficients. We find a similar trend for active and reserve component service members: The cross-sectional coefficient is positive (and around 0.02 to 0.06 across and within services—see Table C.6 in the appendix for by-service results), suggesting each additional four previously completed courses leads to a 20-percent increase in likelihood of a course being taken in this six-month span) and the fixed effect coefficient is negative (at between 0.05 and 0.12; or each additional four courses completed previously leads to about a 30-percent drop in likelihood of a course this six-month period). The cross-sectional result suggests unobserved proclivity for education: The same service member who took more TA in the past is more likely to take it now. The fixed effects estimator with the cumulative is bigger for later years mechanically, so it shows both that if a service member has recently taken

Table 5.11
In-Service Hypothesis 1, National Interrupted Time-Series Regressions, Change in TA Usage for Each Additional Prior Completed TA Course (all services)

	Active	Reserve
Cross-Sectional	0.0541***	0.0272***
	(0.000235)	(0.00113)
Fixed Effects	−0.0640***	−0.0994***
	(0.000441)	(0.00266)

NOTES: ***$p < 0.01$, ** $p < 0.05$, *$p < 0.1$, adjusted for multiple hypotheses.

Standard errors in parentheses. Control variables: post-PGIB, years of service, having dependents, gender, race dummies, cumulative completed courses, high AFQT score, college attainment, age, months deployed in last six months, resident state unemployment rate, service authorized strength, quadratic in years, skill level, month dummies, state dummies, pay status dummies, MOS dummies, service dummies.

more TA, holding her education preferences constant, she is less likely to take more now, and that later in her career, she is less likely to take more TA.

Benefit Usage Hypothesis 2: Effects of PGIB on TA Usage Are More Positive for Those with Dependents

PGIB may be less of a substitute for those with dependents, who may want to use TA for themselves and PGIB for dependents. As such, the positive complementary nature of the programs may dominate more, leading to a positive difference between those with dependents and those without. We run the same regressions as hypothesis 1, except using the difference-in-differences methodology where we interact PGIB with an indicator for having dependents. We use both the cross-sectional approach and the fixed effects approach.

Table 5.12 presents the coefficient on the interaction between after-PGIB and having dependents. We find for the cross-sectional regressions that those with dependents are less responsive to PGIB take-up affecting TA usage. This is contrary to our hypothesis, and it isn't clear why. Service members in the reserve components are more likely to follow the hypothesis. The fixed effects estimators are smaller but similar to the cross-sectional results. Table C.7 in Appendix C presents the results by service. This suggests there is considerable heterogeneity across services in this coefficient.

Benefit Usage Hypothesis 3: Effects of TA Usage and PGIB Take-up on In-Service Promotion is Overall Ambiguous, but More Positive for TA Usage than for PGIB Take-up

We look at how promotion in the military is correlated with TA and PGIB usage. We focus our attention on enlistee promotion to E-5 by three years or by four years (two separate regressions), conditional on still being in the service at the two-year mark. We include those who left the service after two years but before four years to account

Table 5.12
In-Service Hypothesis 2: Difference-in-Differences Regressions, Differential Change in TA Usage from Passage of PGIB for Those with Dependents (all services)

	Active	Reserve
Cross-Sectional	−0.0346***	0.106***
	(0.00591)	(0.0345)
Fixed Effects	−0.0316***	0.0942
	(0.00934)	(0.0580)

NOTES: ***$p < 0.01$, **$p < 0.05$, *$p < 0.1$, adjusted for multiple hypotheses.

Standard errors in parentheses. Control variables: post-PGIB, years of service, having dependents, gender, race dummies, cumulative completed courses, high AFQT score, college attainment, age, months deployed in past six months, resident state unemployment rate, service authorized strength, quadratic in years, skill level, month dummies, state dummies, pay status dummies, MOS dummies, service dummies.

for those who were not progressing or being promoted and left as a result. There is one observation per service member, so we cannot do fixed effects regressions, and we have no difference-in-differences approach here. We include as many controls as we can: in addition to the covariate of interest (an indicator for whether any TA had been completed up to that point), we also include individual covariates (having dependents, high AFQT score, service entry college experience, race, gender, number of months deployed over the last six months, skill level, occupation, and age), service covariates (authorized strength), geographic controls (state indicator, state unemployment rate), and time variables (month indicators and quadratic in date).

It is unclear whether the effect should be positive or negative. Higher TA and PGIB use may be correlated with academic quality, which would make service members more likely to exit after their first contract to use PGIB and get a degree. On the other hand, conditional on staying, service members may be more likely to be promoted because of underlying unobserved (to the econometrician) quality correlated with TA and PGIB use. For TA, use may also serve as a signal of quality to those making the promotion decisions. For PGIB use, it is unobserved until after the service member leaves the military, so it cannot be factored in as a signal used by the service members.

Although we have ambiguous hypotheses for TA and PGIB overall, we do expect the coefficient on TA use to be more positive than the coefficient for PGIB. This is true for two reasons. First, TA is both a signal and a correlate with quality, while PGIB is just a correlate with quality. The signaling aspect of TA may make the coefficient more positive. Second, insofar as completing TA during service is more difficult than completing education using PGIB after service, it may be more correlated with high-quality service members and, thus, yield a more positive coefficient.

Table 5.13 presents the regression coefficients on TA and PGIB take-up. The results are in line with our hypotheses, and we find that the effect that seems to dominate is the correlation with unobserved quality and signaling. The coefficients are generally positive. TA contains both a signal to superiors of effort and quality and a correlation of unobserved (to the econometrician) quality, while PGIB usage contains only the latter. Both may be correlated with being more likely to leave, but we find that service members are promoted anyway or that the promotion effect dominates. The effects are not particularly small: for TA usage, promotion to E-5 by four years for all services, using TA is correlated with almost a 7–percentage point increase in the likelihood of the promotion. PGIB's effect, which does not contain the signal, is about one-fifth the size on average of the TA, which contains the signal. This may be due to TA usage being a stronger correlate with underlying quality (more difficult to do TA during service than PGIB after service) as well as TA usage serving as a signal to superiors regarding effort and quality. Table C.8 in the appendix presents the by-service versions of this model.

Benefit Usage Hypothesis 4: TA Usage Has an Ambiguous Effect on PGIB Take-up

It is unclear ex-ante what effect TA usage should have on PGIB take-up. On one hand, the two may be positively correlated because of unobserved ability that affects both. On the other hand, the two may be negatively related because they are substitutes. This is closely related to the question we investigated earlier for benefits hypothesis 1, where we focused on how passage of PGIB affected TA use. Now, we look instead at actual PGIB take-up, which allows us to focus more closely on the contrasting substitute and complement story by highlighting veterans who go on to use the PGIB benefits.

We investigate the question by regressing PGIB take-up for their own education on TA usage during their career with other controls. We limit the regression to service

Table 5.13
In-Service Hypothesis 3: Regression Results, Effect of TA and PGIB Usage on Promotion Tempo (all services)

	TA	PGIB
Promote to E-5 at 3 years	0.0256***	0.00476***
	(0.000634)	(0.000439)
Promote to E-5 at 4 years	0.0692***	0.0146***
	(0.00119)	(0.000855)

NOTES: TA: Regression coefficients on having taken TA during service. PGIB: Regression coefficient postservice on taking up PGIB.

***$p < 0.01$, **$p < 0.05$, *$p < 0.1$, adjusted for multiple hypotheses. Standard errors in parentheses. Control variables: post-PGIB, years of service, having dependents, gender, race dummies, cumulative completed courses, high AFQT score, college attainment, age, months deployed in past six months, resident state unemployment rate, service authorized strength, quadratic in years, skill level, month dummies, state dummies, pay status dummies, MOS dummies, service dummies.

members who exit the military at least two years prior to our observation of PGIB take-up in September 2015. We include the following individual controls: having dependents, gender, age, race, high AFQT, service entry education, terminal skill level, pay, years of service prior to separation, and MOS occupation. We include unemployment rate in their state when they exit the military. We also include a quadratic in the date of their separation.

We find a coefficient of 0.0105, statistically significant at the 1-percent level. The effect that dominates is the correlation with quality and use of PGIB and TA as complements. However, the magnitude is small. Service members who used TA during their service are about 1 percentage point more likely to use PGIB within two years after separation for their own education. While this effect is small, it is precisely estimated even after controlling for multiple hypotheses. Table C.9 reports the results by service. The results are very similar across the services.

Summary of Findings

Overall, we find that the passage of PGIB had very modest effects on enlistment and retention decisions. For enlistment, we find small and positive to no effects of PGIB on quality of enlistees. The strongest identification strategy from the WGIB benefits shows no statistically significant results, while the more general but weaker identified results from the national interrupted time-series shows small but positive and significant effects on average quality of enlistees, with larger effects in the Army. These results hold for several different measures of quality. The results are slightly larger for those in the reserve components versus those in the active component.

As for retention, there is consistent evidence that the education benefits were associated with about a 1– to 3–percentage point drop in overall continuation rates. The effect was largest on longer-horizon continuation (past seven years more than past five). There is consistent evidence that those with dependents had a smaller drop in continuation rates from the expanded education benefits, at about half the size.

Finally, for education benefit usage, we find that passage of PGIB induced service members to take slightly more courses through TA. We find about a 15-percent increase in likelihood of taking a TA course in the past six months after PGIB. There is weaker, but some, evidence that those with dependents are less responsive to changing TA after PGIB. Both TA and PGIB take-up increase the rate of promotion, with TA having a larger effect, suggesting that TA and PGIB serve both as signals of effort and quality and as a covariate with unobserved (to the econometrician) quality that also affects promotion. In addition, we find higher TA usage is correlated with higher PGIB take-up. In the next chapter, we present some additional contextual information to describe what service members and potential service members know about education benefits, as well as their plans for the future.

CHAPTER SIX

Other Sources of Information: Search Data, Survey Data

The previous chapters describe our main results. They are based on both qualitative and quantitative data. We held focus groups to collect qualitative data about new recruits' knowledge of and plans to use education benefits. We also obtained quantitative data from several different sources and used this information and econometric models to estimate the extent to which the passage of the PGIB affected recruiting and retention. While these sources of data provide detailed information about key phases in each service member's career, it would be helpful to have additional information on other aspects of service members' careers and decisionmaking. In this chapter, we briefly discuss other types of data that have the potential to reveal additional useful information. We focus on two separate sources of data—Internet search data and data from a large, periodic DoD survey of service members. Search data can help us understand the questions and interests of people considering military service. Here, we emphasize the questions that pertain to education benefits. Survey data can reveal information about service members' future plans; we focus on questions that involve education benefits. We discuss each source of data in turn.

Internet Search Data

The Internet has become an indispensable part of everyday life, with Internet searches enabling people to discover new ideas and learn new things. Trillions of web searches are conducted worldwide every year. The data collected by search engines such as Google or Yahoo! constitute a source of information that can be used to supplement other more traditional sources.

Among the set of search engines, Google is the clear leader: It accounts for 90 percent of all worldwide queries and nearly three-quarters of U.S. searches (StatCounter data quoted in Search Engine Watch, 2015). Google collects data on the prevalence of search queries (key words entered into its search engine) across time and geography and makes these terms available to the public. Tools such as Google Trends and Google AdWords provide anonymous and aggregated data on how frequently keywords or phrases have been queried over a specific period of time or within a specific geographic location.[1]

Of course, such data have downsides—in particular, Internet search data are anonymous, and the data exist in aggregated form. Thus, we may be able to understand a great deal about what is searched, but we have little information about who is doing the searching. (We can examine searches by geographic region and date/time; in some cases this reveals information about the searchers). Despite the anonymous format of these data, measures of search intensity have been linked to a number of relevant outcomes.[2]

Next, we collect and classify information on military-relevant searches. Finally, we link search data to data on applicants and accessions to test the hypothesis that search data could be used to increase the predictive power of recruiting-type models.

Internet Queries by Service

One of the more powerful uses of Internet search query data is the analysis of lexical content. In this section we compile a list of the most commonly asked military-relevant questions, by service. To categorize the top searches by service, we used the Keyword Planner tool in Google AdWords.[3]

A few themes emerge from these top questions. While pay-related searches occur frequently, some of the top service-related searches are not related to enlistment at all. For example, two of the top Army-related searches concern other countries' armed forces. Within the Navy-related searches, SEAL-related searches are dominant. This is interesting given that the SEALS are a small group, making up less than 1 percent of all active component Navy personnel. However, the SEALS have appeared prominently in popular culture over the last decade.[4] To fully investigate the content of the questions in each service, we next divide the entire list of questions into the following broad categories:

- General: These searches are often related to the functions of the service, or to specific jobs.
- Pay-Benefits: These searches are related to various aspects of compensation.

---

[1]   See Appendix D for additional information about Google Trends and Google AdWords.

[2]   Examples include monthly unemployment reports (Ettredge, Gerdes, and Karuga, 2005), flu outbreaks (Ginsberg et al., 2009), volatility of the leading stock market index (Dimpfl and Jank, 2015), and the proportion of highly qualified Army accessions (Jahedi, Wenger, and Yeung, 2016).

[3]   Within Google AdWords, we identified the absolute number of searches that contain the name of each service (i.e., Army, Navy, Air Force, or Marines) as well as any of the following keywords: "who," "what," "where," "when," "why," "how," "which," "do," "can," "has," "did," "is," "was," "will," "does," "should," and "could."

[4]   For example, SEALS have appeared in movies, books, and video games. The involvement of Navy SEALS in the operation that resulted in the capture and death of Osama bin Laden was widely publicized, and searches related to the Navy SEALS peaked sharply in May 2011, concurrent with this operation.

- Procedures: These searches request information about enlistment.
- Qualifications: This category includes a wide variety of questions related to qualifications to enlist; topics include age requirements, health-related requirements, questions related to past drug and alcohol use, questions about disqualification due to existing criminal records, and a variety of other questions.
- Education: This category includes all questions about education; some searches inquire about whether the services pay for enlistees to attend college, while others focus on education requirements to enlist.
- Other: This category consists of searches that are not related to enlistment (such as searches concerning other countries' armed forces). These make up 15 to 19 percent of the total searches for each service; we exclude these searches from the remainder of our analyses.

Dividing the searches in this manner allows us to compare the types of questions asked by service. Sorting the searches into categories involves some judgment, so we developed and tested a protocol for consistent sorting.[5]

The breakdown of questions by category for each service is depicted in Figure 6.1. For comparison purposes, we include military-related questions as well as service-specific ones. Search patterns differ across the services. For most services, questions in the "General" category are prevalent. (The exception is the Air Force, where "Pay-Benefits" searches are slightly more common.) Among the services, questions involving pay, benefits, and procedures are more common than searches related to the military as a whole. It seems plausible that searchers begin with general military searches, and then progress to service-specific searches, although these data do not allow us to test this hypothesis. Across the services, education-related searches are unusual. This suggests that at least initially, many of the searches that involve aspects of enlistment do not focus on education or education benefits. Indeed, searches about pay dominate all searches related to aspects of pay and benefits. In other words, searchers frequently look for information about military pay but search far less frequently for information about benefits (education or otherwise).

Searches related to the military and education benefits do exist. The most common education-related search question is: "does the military pay for college?" But this search term is found far less frequently than terms related to other aspects of service. This does not indicate that benefits are unimportant—but it implies that initial Google searches related to military enlistment are far more likely to include other aspects of service.

---

[5]   We focused on interrater reliability: Two researchers first sorted a portion of the search terms independently, then met to compare their sorting, then discussed and resolved the points of difference, then repeated the process. We were able to achieve agreement on over 98 percent of the searches sorted after the second iteration.

Figure 6.1
Most Common Searches, by Service and Category

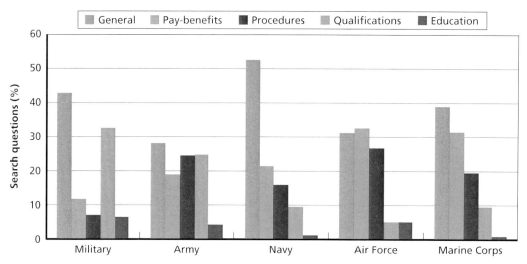

SOURCE: RAND NDRI analysis, based on data from Google Adwords, undated.
NOTE: Data from U.S. searches, September 2013–August 2015.
RAND RR1766-6.1

Internet Search Queries and Military Applicants

As discussed previously, a drawback of Internet search data is the anonymous, aggregated nature of the information—we do not know who carried out the search. However, other research has linked search data to a variety of relevant outcomes. In our case, if search data are relevant, we would expect that the data would be predictive of recruitment (if more people are searching for information about recruitment, more people are interested in enlistment and are likely to talk with recruiters and begin the process of applying to enlist). To test this hypothesis, we use a straightforward regression model to examine the relationship between search behavior and applicants.

For consistency, we chose a similar set of search queries for each service. The terms that were chosen are *ASVAB* [Armed Services Vocational Battery], *[service] jobs*, *[service] salary*, and *join [service]*, where [service] denotes each military service respectively: Army, Navy, Air Force, Marines. Our analyses of Internet queries suggests the terms chosen are likely to be searched by those who have interest in joining the service. Our regression models explain the log of high-quality applicants to each branch of the military.[6,7] We include controls for month and year, which account for regular, seasonal

---

[6]   As is typical in the literature, *high-quality* here is defined as having a high school diploma or equivalent credential, *and* scoring above the 50th percentile on the AFQT. See, e.g., Buddin, 2005.

[7]   We focus here on applicants rather than enlistments because we take the view that application can be thought of as a more direct measure of propensity and interest than enlistment. Several steps, and a significant time lag, occur between application and enlistment; also, the services offer significant enlistment bonuses during some

time trends and help to control for other relevant factors (such as the unemployment rate).[8] There is little theoretical justification for including or excluding various search terms in these models, so we include the search queries in the regressions one at a time. Our results indicate that the search term *ASVAB* is highly predictive of changes in the high-quality applicants to each branch of the military, although it varies across the services. For a 10-percent change in the relative search volume of the term *ASVAB*, the percentage of high-quality applicants increases between 7 percent and 10 percent.[9] These results suggest that Internet search data provide information on the overall level of interest in military enlistment. It is possible that such data could be used in addition to more traditional, survey-based measures of propensity in recruiting models, thus producing more robust results.

Queries About the GI Bill

Finally, we analyze the content of questions regarding the GI Bill. In Figure 6.2, we generate a word cloud that visually portrays the most common terms searched (in this case, we examine phrases, rather than single words). It is apparent from Figure 6.2 that many of the inquiries are general in nature, or refer to the value of the benefit or the procedures by which it can be used. Also, many of the questions appear to be close variants of other questions.

To quantify the topics being queried in more detail, we categorize the list of questions into bins and plot the relative frequency of each bin, as we did with more general search terms above. The largest category of searches related to the GI Bill is procedural; this category includes about 40 percent of all searches. Examining individual procedure-related queries suggests that most of these searches were probably carried out by current service members. The next largest category is general questions; these make up just above 30 percent of queries. Another large category is queries related to the value and time period of the benefit; these make up just above 20 percent of all GI Bill–related searches. About 5 percent of all searches involved transferring the PGIB benefit, and about 1 percent specifically involved the housing or living allowance aspect of the benefit. Thus, initial searches for information related to the GI Bill do not commonly

---

time periods but very few bonuses during other periods. Finally, some applicants are not eligible to enlist, and some choose not to enlist (for reasons related to bonuses, availability of training seats, or other factors). Therefore, applicants with similar levels of initial propensity may have a different probability of enlistment, and of accession. While discerning a relationship between enlistments/accessions and search behavior should be more difficult, past research has found that, at least in the case of the Army, lagged searches are related to accessions; see Jahedi, Wenger, and Yeung, 2016.

[8]   Because our models are based on aggregated data, we cannot control for the fiscal year, month, and unemployment rate simultaneously.

[9]   We also include a variable indicating ASVAB searches in the previous month; the coefficient on this variable is smaller than on the current month's ASVAB searches but is statistically significant, suggesting that there is in some cases a lag between searches and applications. For additional information on our regression results, see Appendix D.

Figure 6.2
Searches Related to GI Bill

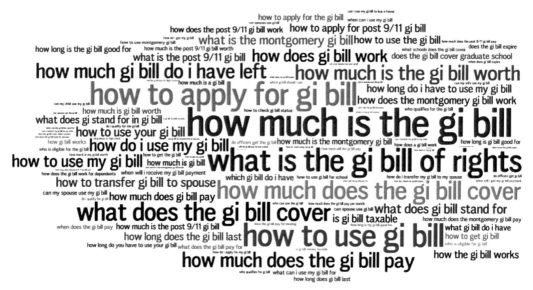

SOURCE: RAND NDRI analysis of Google AdWords data from U.S. searches, May 2013–April 2015. Created using wordle.com.

RAND RR1766-6.2

concern the transfer aspect or the living allowance aspect of the bill, but searches for information about the bill appear quite common.

As people have begun to spend more time online searching for information, Internet search data have become a remarkably rich source of insights regarding people's interests and concerns. We used Google Trends and AdWords—publicly available tools that provide access to Google's search data—to explore attitudes about and interest in joining the military.

Although search data offer many advantages, these data are also subject to certain important limitations; therefore, the results should be interpreted with care. First, information about the population carrying out these searches is not readily available. Although many people use the Internet and search engines, the sample of searchers is not random. For example, someone who searches for information about the military may be a military service member, a person who is considering joining the military, or someone simply curious about the military. There is no way of determining either the intent behind search behavior or population characteristics, such as propensity for military service or enlistment status. Also, our analyses necessarily exclude individuals without Internet access or those who do not use Google as their search engine. Our conclusions are therefore conditional on the population of searchers. Furthermore, individuals differ in their propensity to use a search engine to obtain information. Someone interested in joining the military, for example, may reach out to a friend or recruiter directly to learn more, whereas some people who search for military-related terms can be doing so for completely unrelated reasons.

Another limitation concerns the link between attitudes (e.g., searches for information about the military), and subsequent behavior (e.g., applying to join the military). While predictive models such as the one we constructed attempt to establish a connection between attitudes and behavior, they can do so only in the aggregate. That is, predictive models can only suggest the relative likelihood of military applicants among various groups with certain patterns of search behavior. The models cannot identify specific *individuals* who have expressed interest in military service or taken any steps to join the military. Given these limitations, it is especially encouraging that our search terms are related to applications.

We identified top searches and categorized them according to some aspect of military service: general, pay-benefits, enlistment procedures, qualifications, education, and other. Searches related to military education benefits were relatively rare, suggesting that those searching for initial information tend to focus on other topics. Searches related to the GI Bill can be examined in a similar manner; many of these searchers appear to seek information on the basics of the bill, while few look for information on the housing or transfer aspects of the bill. Next, we utilize data from a large, repeated survey to understand more about current service members' plans to use education benefits.

Education and Service Members' Future Plans

Administrative data from service members' records contains detailed information about service members' careers, and their decisions to join, remain in, or leave the military. However, military policy also has a substantial influence on these decisions; for example, a service member's decision to leave the military may be influenced not only by his or her civilian opportunities but also by actual and perceived probabilities of military promotion. Administrative data do not include information about service members' perceptions or plans. To learn more about service members' plans to use their education benefits, we examine a different source of data. The Status of Forces Survey (SOF) of Active Duty Members is fielded multiple times every year to a random sample of service members and DoD civilian employees.[10, 11] For this analysis, we focus on active component members of the Army, Navy, Air Force, and Marine Corps; we include data from 2002 to 2013.

---

[10] We express our gratitude to Michael DiNicolantonio at DMDC for assisting us in acquiring and understanding these data.

[11] The SOF is a web-based survey conducted by the Human Resources Strategic Assessment Program (HRSAP) and DMDC to support personnel needs of the USD (P&R). For additional information about the SOF, see Appendix E.

Some of the questions in the SOF surveys stay the same, while others change over time. Here, we focus on a small subset of questions that are consistent over time and pertinent to service members' future plans for educational attainment.

Description of Analyses

We focus on the following questions:

- To what extent did money for college, college repayment, or education contribute to your decision to join?
- Any college credits earned since joining?
- To what extent is continuing your education a reason for your leaving the service within the next two years?
- Has spouse completed bachelor's degree or higher?

We chose these questions because they describe the service member's perceptions of how education benefits influence enlistment, the service member's educational attainment while on active duty, the service member's plans to obtain additional education, and the spouse's level of education (the latter is likely to influence the probability of transferring the PGIB to the spouse).

To analyze the data, we divide or stratify the sample into groups and look for differences across the groups and across time. We stratify all analyses by three levels of (service member) education: high school or less, some college, and a college degree or higher. We also hypothesize that more senior service members will have different reasons and plans for using educational benefits; they are older and more established in their career and, as a result, they may both have a better understanding of their options and different attitudes toward transferring benefits than newer recruits. Additionally, the Post-9/11 GI Bill requires reenlistment to be eligible for spousal and dependent transfers. Stratification by years of service allows for closer estimates of those who may be considering reenlistment. Because of our interest in benefits transfers, a third obvious stratification is between those with and those without dependents. Finally, we examine the data by groups of pay grades. While we expect pay grade to generally be correlated with both education and years of service, there still may be important differences by pay grade that do not show up in the other stratifications. Specifically, pay grade allows for the separation of officers and enlisted, and a hierarchy that may not exactly map to time spent in the military, or education level. In each case, we test for differences within and across the stratified groups, and for differences over time.[12] We hypothesize that service member responses will vary by education, years of service,

---

[12] The responses in the SOF are framed as Likert scales and generally measure level of agreement with the statement. We collapse the data into two categories to capture agreement versus lack of agreement. See Appendix E for more details on our stratified sample, our analytic decisions, and on the statistical tests used to measure differences between groups and over time.

and/or dependent status. Finally, we hypothesize that service members may be more likely to plan to use education benefits after the PGIB was passed; in this case, we would expect to see a change over time.

Results

Here, we summarize our results by question. The results discussed in the text are statistically significant at the 5-percent level or better, indicating such results would occur by chance less than 1 time in 20. In Appendix E, we include specific p-values (the level of significance) for each statistical test and stratification discussed.

To What Extent Did Money for College, College Repayment, or Education Contribute to Your Decision to Join?

Those in junior pay grades, those with college experience, newer recruits, and those with no dependents indicated that money for education had more influence on their decisions than other groups. Over time, those completing the SOF were more likely to indicate that money for college and educational purposes had influenced their decision. In particular, an uptick occurred in 2007, prior to the passage of the PGIB but during an era of sharply increasing college costs.

Any College Credits Earned Since Joining?

Between 2004 and 2012 there was a modest but statistically significant downward trend in the proportion of individuals taking college credits while in the military, except O-4–O-6 officers, who evidenced a slight uptick in college credits earned. On average, those in lower pay grades and with fewer years of service, as well as those with no dependents, were significantly less likely than others to earn credits. This change could also be related to the intensive deployment cycles, changes in service policies concerning TA, and/or potential changes in the promotion process over the last decade.

To What Extent Is Continuing Your Education a Reason for Your Leaving the Service Within the Next Two Years?

As for stating plans to leave the service to pursue educational opportunities, there were major differences between our subgroups. Those with fewer years of service, those in the junior enlisted pay grades, and individuals without dependents were much more likely to indicate such plans. For example, in 2011, nearly half of the E-1–E-4 pay grade members answered affirmatively; these answers differ significantly from those of more senior enlisted personnel, or officers. Of course, the difference between junior enlisted and senior officers is not unexpected. The gap between those with dependents and no dependents widened over time; while both groups were more likely to indicate plans to attend, this result is consistent with some service members planning to remain in service to secure benefits for their dependents.

Has Spouse Completed Bachelors' Degree or Higher?

There was a small but significant trend toward more educated spouses between 2003 and 2006. On average, individuals with higher pay grades, years of service, and education had more educated spouses. More junior service members typically had less educated partners

The SOF data indicate that some service members' enlistment decisions were influenced by the availability of educational funds. This is especially true among service members in junior pay grades and those with some college experience. These results match reasonably well with what we heard in our focus groups. SOF data also indicate that those who have no dependents were more likely to indicate the influence of educational funds. This trend was not discernable in our focus groups. Finally, the SOF data suggest that many service members indicated the importance of educational benefits prior to the passage of the PGIB, but service members were more likely to report being influenced by educational benefits beginning in 2007. It is not clear that this trend was driven by the PGIB, but the increasing costs of college during this time period could help to explain it.

Service members today report taking fewer college courses while on active duty than in the past. Many service members report that continuing their education poses a likely reason for leaving the military in the near future, but there is no evidence of a large increase over time. Finally, service members' spouses are more likely to have completed college today than in the past. This shift, however, appears to have occurred before the PGIB was passed. To summarize the most relevant of these results, service members often indicated that education benefits had been a factor in their enlistment decisions, and that they were likely to leave the military to attend college in the near future. However, these answers were more prevalent among some groups than others; young service members and enlisted service members were more likely than others to indicate agreement. There were some increases in agreement over time, but it is not clear that the increases in agreement necessarily track the passage of the PGIB. Service members indicated the importance of education benefits, even before the passage of the PGIB.

CHAPTER SEVEN

Conclusions and Recommendations

Service members have access to a variety of education benefits throughout and after their military careers. Prior research has documented the positive impacts of military service and these programs in particular on educational attainment and civilian earnings, but there is less existing research documenting whether and how these programs could be used to serve force management goals. In this report, we address this research gap by examining the ways in which the two largest education benefits programs—the PGIB and TA—are likely to influence recruiting and retention. We explicitly recognize that these programs are valuable to service members and are likely to improve their eventual labor market outcomes and perhaps even their levels of job satisfaction, job match, and other relevant outcomes. However, our focus here is on specific aspects of force management—recruitment and retention—and how education benefits are likely to influence these aspects of force management. We also examine the interaction between PGIB and TA.

Our report is organized around the trajectory of a service member's career, and around three primary research questions:

1. How do military education benefits influence recruiting?
2. How to do military education benefits influence retention?
3. To what extent do military personnel use the TA and PGIB programs separately or together to further their education?

To address these research questions, we used a broad mixed-methods approach informed by a conceptual model. In this way, we are able to include information about the level of knowledge, usage, and plans for usage that service members have at various stages of their careers, as well as measures of retention and benefit use. Such information is important for developing informed hypotheses about the likely impact of the passage of the PGIB on recruitment and retention outcomes. For example, if recruits have little knowledge about the expansion of benefits that came with the passage of the PGIB, then we should not expect to see a large impact of PGIB passage on recruitment. Similarly, the level of awareness about the details for transferring benefits to dependents would inform our expectations about likely effects of transferability on retention.

Thus, while our study relies primarily upon quantitative methods to assess the impact of the passage of the PGIB on recruitment and retention, we use qualitative methods to inform our hypotheses and provide important context to the quantitative findings.

Moreover, as discussed in the opening chapters of this report, the passage of the PGIB represents a large change to education benefits available, but all service members received the new benefit in 2009, and many other relevant changes were occurring at the same time. Additionally, the period since 2009 generally has been characterized as a period of positive recruiting. This somewhat limits our ability to assess the over- all impact of PGIB passage on these outcomes using rigorous quantitative methods. This fact underscores the importance of our mixed-methods approach, which allows us to triangulate findings from a variety of quantitative and qualitative approaches to develop informed and nuanced conclusions that stand up to multiple methods. In the next sections we revisit our qualitative and quantitative results; we then summarize the evidence we have gathered on recruitment and retention; we close with a discussion of the implications and recommendations flowing from our research.

New Recruits' Knowledge of, and Plans for, Education Benefits

We carried out focus groups across the country, including newly enlisted members of each service. While recruits have varied and often limited levels of knowledge about the specifics of education benefits, they are generally aware of the existence of these benefits and often state that they plan to use them. This suggests that a general aware- ness of benefits, rather than consideration of specific restrictions or benefit components, is likely to be driving enlistment decisions. The few recruits who were well informed about military education benefits appeared to be older, more likely to have prior experi- ence with college, more likely to be female, and less likely to be entering the Marines. In many cases, recruits do not understand how the current PGIB benefits differ from those offered under the MGIB. Based on this, we would expect to find only a muted response, if any, to the increase in benefits that the PGIB represents. It is possible that with more emphasis on education benefits during the recruiting process, the recruiting response would be more apparent.

Veterans and Service Members as Students: Insights from Interviews with College Counselors

We carried out a small number of interviews with student advisors at colleges across the United States. The results of these interviews suggest that military and veteran student offices play a key role in supporting military and veteran students. Those inter- viewed indicated that even after enrolling, some military and veteran students still lack detailed knowledge about their education benefits. In particular, they lack understanding of the underlying procedures and requirements related to the PGIB. Advisors also indicated that many of these students do not think strategically about how to utilize their various benefits and combine them effectively with other sources of support. While current service members using the TA program seemed generally well informed, the complex nature of PGIB benefits and a perceived lack of guidance from military sources may continue to present a significant challenge to veteran students.

Other Sources of Qualitative Information

We also drew upon Internet search data and survey information to provide richer qualitative data on service member knowledge about and use of education benefits. Internet search data suggest that education-related searches are relatively rare among those who initially seek information about enlistment; this suggests that education benefits may not be a major driver in attracting initial interest in military enlistment.

To understand how service members plan to use their education benefits, we analyzed multiple waves of data collected over a decade through the SOF surveys. Over time, those completing the survey have become more likely to indicate that money for college played a role in their initial decision to join the military. This may reflect the recent increases in the cost of college. Junior service members were more likely than senior service members to indicate that they intended to pursue college as a primary activity after leaving the military; this effect is especially pronounced among those with dependents. Most time trends were modest in nature; in particular, there was a modest increase in the level of spousal education, and a small decrease in the proportion earning college credit while in the military. These data span the period before and after passage of the PGIB.

How Did Service Members' Quality and Retention Rates Change After the PGIB?

Our quantitative results are based on administrative data and on models that estimate the number and proportion of high-quality enlistees, as well as continuation rates. We estimate cross-service models but also estimate many models separately by service and allow for differences between the active and reserve components. We estimate and compare results across a number of different subgroups; in particular, we examine those with and without children, as well as service members in states with programs that resemble some parts of the PGIB versus service members in surrounding states that lack such programs.

In terms of recruit quality, the majority (but not all) of our models indicate that the proportion of high-quality recruits increased after the PGIB was passed, and that a portion of the increase does not seem to be linked to other factors (such as the civilian economy). We find generally similar results when we examine other measures related to quality. Our continuation models find that continuation did decrease after the passage of the PGIB, and that some of the decrease cannot be explained by other factors (such as the civilian economy). We also find that holding other factors constant, the decrease in continuation was smaller among those with dependents than among service members without dependents. This is consistent with the intent of the transfer aspect of the PGIB.

Finally, we find evidence that TA and the PGIB appear to work in concert. Even after the passage of the PGIB, service members have continued to use TA. Indeed, passage of the PGIB is associated with a small increase in TA usage. In this context, TA could represent an opportunity for those service members who choose to attend a four-year college on the PGIB to increase the probability of completing a degree within the confines of their PGIB benefits. The PGIB provides 36 months of benefits; this is sufficient for four years of study at nine months per year, but recent cohorts have been unlikely to complete a degree in this time period (Cataldi et al., 2011), and a student who transfers is less likely than others to complete a degree within a four-year window. Thus, using TA to obtain some credits is likely to provide a buffer against unexpected setbacks and, therefore, to increase the probability of completing a degree.

In Chapter Five, we provided additional detail on the costs associated with TA and PGIB, and we provided estimates of the cost per semester of credit. In short, TA is less costly than the PGIB, but those using the PGIB have already completed many more estimated semesters of credit than those using TA.

We find that those who use TA and/or PGIB are more likely than others to be promoted. The PGIB result is especially interesting, as the promotion in question occurs prior to the use of the PGIB. TA and PGIB could attract more productive service members, increase these service members' productivity, or serve as a signal of service members' commitments (or some combination of these effects).

Next, we summarize all the aspects of our study that relate to recruiting, then the aspects related to retention. Finally, we discuss overall implications and recommendations.

Summarizing the Evidence: Recruiting

Our national models, and some state models, indicate a statistically significant increase in the quality of enlistees after passage of the PGIB. The size of the effect, across the services, is small; for example, we estimate that the proportion of service members meeting the *high-quality* standard increased from 70 percent to 71 percent after the

PGIB passed. The size of the effect is not surprising, given our qualitative findings—new enlistees understand that the military offers education benefits, but they lack a nuanced or detailed understanding of the PGIB (and they have very little knowledge of TA). For this reason, although the shift from the MGIB to the PGIB represents a substantial increase in benefit generosity, most new service members have only a limited understanding of the extent to which the PGIB (versus the MGIB) covers college costs. It is possible that further educating potential recruits about various aspects of the PGIB could create a situation in which the bill had a larger impact on recruit quality, but we have no direct evidence of this. It is also possible that in other recruiting conditions (such as a different civilian economy, coupled with a lower probability of deployment and/or continuing growth in the cost of college), service members might value the bill differently. Although a positive recruiting environment prevailed during the final years included in our study, our data include some variation in terms of economic conditions, and the results we find are consistently quite small.

Summarizing the Evidence: Retention

As is the case for recruiting, the retention effects of the PGIB appear to be fairly small. Continuation rates appear to have decreased 2 to 3 percentage points in response to the passage of the PGIB. Some state models show similar effects. Service members with dependents have a smaller response—in the neighborhood of 1– to 1.5–percentage point decrease in continuation. While survey data indicate that many service members plan to use their education benefits, and a substantial proportion plan to attend college full time after leaving the military, our interviews with college counselors suggest that many who leave the military and begin school still lack a complete understanding of the PGIB.

Implications and Recommendations

TA and the PGIB are large and expensive programs; our study and many other studies suggest that they result in substantial accumulation of human capital by current and former service members. However, from the perspective of recruiting and retention, the effect of the passage of the PGIB in particular appears to have been relatively small. Evidence from across our data sources consistently suggests that service members and veterans lack a complete and nuanced understanding of the PGIB, especially of the differences between the PGIB and the previous education benefit. This is the most likely explanation for the muted effects of the PGIB passage on recruiting in particular; new recruits frequently do not understand basic aspects of this benefit, and especially do not understand the ways in which the PGIB differs from previous education benefits available to service members. One reason for the lack of nuanced understanding may lie in the bill's construction; it is a complex benefit. For example, the transfer of a portion of one's PGIB benefit to a dependent must occur prior to leaving the services. What is clear is that our qualitative data suggest that most recruits do have a general understanding that the military will cover the majority of their educational expenses. The fact that this was generally true before the PGIB went into effect is a likely explanation for the relatively muted effects of the PGIB on recruitment. The effects on retention are relatively modest as well, suggesting that service members also consider other factors when deciding whether to remain in the military.

The muted effects of this bill's passage on recruiting and retention suggest that, all else equal, modest changes to the benefit are likely to have even smaller impacts on recruiting and retention. The PGIB represents (on average) a substantial increase in funds available for educational pursuits, but passage of the PGIB resulted in quite small changes in recruit quality and continuation/retention. Therefore, any future adjustments to the PGIB (in either direction) that constitute smaller changes than the original passage would be expected to result in smaller changes to recruiting and retention than did the original passage.

As a complex benefit, the PGIB has many aspects that could be changed. For example, the years of service required for the transfer benefit could be increased. We have no direct data comparing take-up of the transfer aspect of the bill under different service requirements, but increasing the level of service is likely to have several effects: First, service members would be more likely to use the bill themselves (less likely to transfer the benefits); this would be expected to cause a small decrease in retention at the current point of transfer. However, such a change would also be likely to lead to a slight increase in retention at the new point required for transfer. In other words, should the years of service required to transfer be increased to something beyond ten years, we expect the retention rates beyond ten years would increase, and thus the experience level of senior personnel would increase. We expect both changes would be small (recall the small change in retention associated with the passage of the bill; again, a change to the bill is likely to lead to effect sizes smaller than the effects associated with passage). Finally, retention rates currently are quite high past ten years; this, too, suggests that any effects due to alterations to the bill would likely be small.

Of course, it is impossible to hold "all else equal" if the PGIB is cut even modestly. Indeed, it would be reasonable to anticipate significant negative media attention surrounding any such changes. To the extent that accompanying media effects alter the perceptions of recruits about the level of generosity of education benefits they could obtain from military service, we might expect a larger negative effect on recruitment than our data would suggest. Nevertheless, we maintain that any negative effects of modest reductions in the PGIB on recruitment and retention are likely to be small and could be offset using more traditional and effective force management tools like enlistment and reenlistment bonuses. Finally, given the likely growth in costs of education benefits programs (particularly the PGIB) in future years, policymakers should consider ways to rein in costs without substantially reducing the value of benefits to service members moving forward. We note that a number of the specific recommendations we have made would also help to reduce the overall cost burden of military education benefits programs.

Following, we make policy recommendations based upon our research findings. Our recommendations fall into two broad categories: (1) recommendations intended to improve information and knowledge about or use of education benefits, and (2) recommendations related to force management; we also provide some suggestions for areas that would be appropriate focuses of future research.

Recommendations Related to Knowledge and Use of Education Benefits

1. *Provide (additional) information to service members at key points in time.* For example, it may make sense to provide additional or more targeted information on education benefits to potential recruits, and/or to provide key information about transfer options and requirements to service members nearing transfer eligibility. We recognize that multiple sources of information about education benefits already exist. Despite this, we find evidence that service members do not understand or appreciate the details of the existing education benefits programs. New enlistees, for example, lack detailed knowledge about the PGIB and appear to have very little knowledge about TA. However, this group does understand that education benefits exist; some new recruits appear to possess more detailed information about the PGIB, and those recruits also appear to have more detailed plans for using their education benefits. It is possible, although not certain, that providing additional information about education benefits to potential recruits could increase their appreciation of these benefits. Under such circumstances, it is possible that education benefits could have a larger influence on potential recruits' enlistment decisions.

Over time, service members appear to gain substantial understanding of education benefit programs. Our interviews with a small number of college advisors, however, suggest that even at the point of enrollment, some service members lack a detailed understanding of some of the key details of the PGIB. Providing additional information to service members considering leaving the military, and/or to those in the process of leaving the military, could be helpful, as could providing targeted information to service members as they become eligible to transfer the benefit. Counseling for first-time PGIB users could pay dividends; we recommend expanding this counseling or making it mandatory. Our qualitative data suggest that recruits have very little knowledge about the details of the education benefits programs available to them. It is also rare for users, and exceedingly so for recruits, to have a specific plan for using their education benefits to meet their education and career goals. Lack of information and planning for education can lead to significant struggles in completing key education credentials, and to inefficient course-taking patterns costly to both the student and the military. Under such circumstances, counseling could assist service members in planning the most effective pathways to achieve their desired educational goals.

Expanding and continuing to fine-tune the existing GI Bill Comparison Tool could also be a way of providing additional information. The GI Bill Comparison Tool was developed through a partnership between VA, DoD, and the Department of Education; the tool provides a wide variety of information helpful to service members and dependents as they search for appropriate postsecondary institutions. The tool draws on rich administrative data from all three agencies to provide information that can help service members and dependent beneficiaries search for appropriate colleges to utilize their benefits. The tool includes useful information about completion rates of different credentials and earnings of graduates at eligible institutions. Such information can be helpful in choosing appropriate programs that can allow service members to complete useful credentials in a timely manner; therefore, this tool has the *potential* to lower costs. Efforts to assess or improve the extent to which service members are aware of this information could pay dividends.

Along with providing additional information, we would recommend careful tracking of the information provided, as well as using a variety of techniques (such as online surveys) to determine how well service members retain the information.

2. *Encourage use of TA program.* We estimate the number of semesters of credit earned and cost per credit hour through the PGIB and TA. The primary takeaway from this analysis is that the cost to the military (the services or VA) of delivering a credit hour of postsecondary education through TA is, on average, substantially lower than the cost of delivering a credit hour via PGIB. While there are a number of reasons for this, the primary one is that PGIB is generally used after separation from service and includes a living stipend for users not currently enlisted or married to and living with a partner currently enlisted. The tuition limits on the PGIB are much higher than those placed on TA, and this, too, plays a role in the cost difference. The government *may* thus be able to achieve cost savings by encouraging more use of TA benefits. It appears that service members use TA to take introductory courses, perhaps in preparation for additional, more-advanced coursework. Especially if future research determines that service members and dependents using PGIB have difficulty completing a course of study or degree, this suggests that encouraging use of TA would also be sensible—in this case, using TA might not lower overall costs but could easily lower the expected costs of degree completion.

Recommendations Related to Force Management Objectives

1. *Continue to focus on traditional force management tools like bonuses—as opposed to education benefits—to achieve force management objectives.* The results of our study suggest that the current education benefits programs are very blunt instruments for achieving force management objectives. The PGIB does appear to attract additional high-quality recruits; the PGIB also appears to decrease retention (although the effect is smaller for service members with children, suggesting that the transfer aspect of the benefit serves to retain some service members). Given the modest size of these effects, we recommend that policymakers focus on other tools, such as bonuses, to achieve force management objectives. And, given the small size of these effects, modest changes to the programs are unlikely to result in meaningful changes in recruitment or reenlistment patterns. Thus, education benefits programs should not be viewed primarily as force management tools. Note that this conclusion does not in any way discount the value of education benefits programs. As we have pointed out, the primary objectives of these programs is and always has been to help service members transition to civilian life and to compensate them for their time in service.

2. *Continue to carefully track recruit quality and retention metrics.* Such metrics are tracked as a matter of course, and, given the modest size of our estimates, we do not expect to see large changes in recruiting or retention metrics in response to any changes to education benefits programs. But especially if there are sudden changes to the PGIB, or to the cost of college, tracking any shifts in recruit quality or retention behavior will be key. Should such shifts occur, our analyses suggest that adjusting standard force management tools (such as bonuses) will be helpful in maintaining quality.

3. *Carefully calibrate alignment between DoD and VA on changes to the PGIB.* Carefully coordinating any changes to the PGIB could assist DoD and the services in obtaining their goals related to recruitment and retention. At present, it is not clear that specific mechanisms for calibration are in place.

Recommendations for Future Research

We also have several suggestions for areas appropriate for future research efforts. First, achieving a better understanding of service members' educational experiences is likely to require data from a variety of sources—both administrative files (such as those kept by the VA) and information from service members themselves. Therefore, we suggest that future research *invest in multimethod approaches to better understand service members' experience with education benefits, and the extent to which they are achieving their primary objectives.* We have noted throughout this document that our data do not allow us to determine which service members and dependents complete degrees or programs;

this information would be extremely helpful in making more overarching determinations of the effectiveness of these programs. But beyond these basic degree completion statistics, additional information about how service members learn about education benefits and how they use education benefits to transition into the civilian sector would be helpful. The higher education landscape is changing rapidly, especially in terms of for-profit providers and overall costs, with all schools coming under pressure to justify costs. Given this, understanding how many service members work in occupations that allow them to use their education, and the longer-term effects of education benefits on educational attainment and on eventual civilian earnings, would be helpful information to determine more about how to improve the programs. Such information could also be quite helpful in determining the best time period(s) to provide service members with additional information about education benefits.

Second, costs of college, and of the PGIB, are considerable. Because of the transfer aspect of the PGIB, decisions today frequently result in costs that will accrue far in the future. Therefore, we suggest that efforts to *forecast costs of education benefits moving forward* will be especially valuable for future planning. Indeed, an important consideration for future policy decisions around military education benefits should be the overall costs of providing those benefits. By all measures, these are high. The current annual cost of the PGIB alone is more than $10 billion (the expenditures on the TA program are much smaller; our data indicate expenditures of more than $300 million in recent years). Moreover, it is important to note that annual PGIB costs will continue to rise as youth dependents who have received transfer benefits begin to enroll in college and draw benefits. It is beyond the scope of the current project to estimate the total costs of these benefits over time, but future work should do so.

More generally, given the anticipated costs of the primary education benefits programs moving forward, it is important to consider potential ways to reduce those costs without significantly hampering the programs' capacity to meet the primary objectives of helping service members achieve their educational goals and smoothing their transition to the civilian world. A number of the recommendations made above, particularly those related to improving information about and usage of benefits, also may have the potential to help bend the cost curve on these programs. For example, encouraging more usage of TA benefits could help to reduce PGIB costs if service members earn a larger share of college credits via TA. Similarly, educational counseling and information tools have the potential to help service members to navigate the complex process of choosing college majors, taking appropriate courses, and transferring them from one institution to another to obtain their desired education more efficiently and effectively—and reducing overall costs. While these recommendations may help to address these issues, more research is needed to identify ways to ensure that service members can use education benefits to efficiently navigate complex degree pathways and reduce the cost burden of education benefits programs.

In closing, this research suggests that the passage of the PGIB has had small impacts on recruiting and retention. We also find evidence that PGIB and TA work together. While these findings indicate that more traditional force management tools like bonuses will continue to offer the most effective and targeted ways to achieve force shaping objectives, our research does not address or question the value of education benefits programs to service members or their potential to smooth service member transitions from military service to the civilian world.

Taken together, our findings suggest that DoD should make every reasonable effort to ensure that education benefits are used in ways that advance service members' careers in the military and beyond. Doing so will create benefits for DoD, will assist service members in reaching their full potential, and will ensure that education benefits are used in a manner consistent with their design.

Detailed Overview of Education Benefits Available to Service Members and Veterans

Overview of Education Benefits

Since the passage of the original GI Bill (Pub. L. 78-346, 1944), each generation of U.S. service members has had a version of a benefits package offered that assisted with the pursuit of higher education, generally following active military service. As volunteer status, force levels, characteristics of service, and economic conditions fluctuated, the generosity and flexibility of the programs fluctuated as well.

DoD, VA, and the Department of Education (ED) administer a variety of programs that provide educational assistance to active-duty and reserve component service members, both before and after their departure from the armed forces. These programs range from examinations that provide college credit for knowledge and experience gained in the military to various kinds of tuition assistance and student aid. The American Council on Education (ACE) College Credit for Military Service program helps service members and veterans transfer college credit earned in the military and earn appropriate credit for military training and experience. Additionally, the Joint Service Transcript program is single-source, lifetime documentation of all military training, schooling, and experience that veterans can use to apply for credit transfer. Figure A.1 is a visual depiction of all oversight authorities and eligibility horizons over the various "phases" of a benefits user's lifespan.

Individuals may be eligible for other private or public benefits not represented in this figure, including assistance provided by state governments, private foundations, colleges and universities, and civilian employers. The color of each program corresponds with the government department (DoD, VA, or ED) that administers and sets policy for a given program. The points in time marked in red highlight significant milestones for a military service member, either the point when he/she joins the military or transitions to a different, post–active-duty service category such as a veteran or Drilling Reserve member. The length of each bar notionally represents the period of time that an individual could be eligible for a program—actual proportional length, of course, will depend on the length of a service career and individual lifetime.

Figure A.1
Organizational Oversight and Individual Lifetime Eligibility Requirements for Federal Educational Assistance Programs

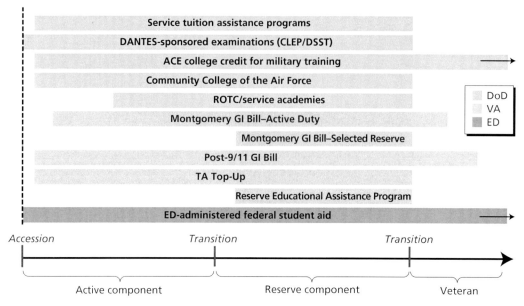

SOURCE: Buryk et al., 2015, Figure 4.1
NOTE: Active component members may transition directly to veteran status, and reserve component members may not have prior active component service. Reserve component members may accrue Montgomery GI Bill–Active Duty or Post-9/11 GI Bill for qualifying service on active duty. Tuition Assistance Top Up benefits may be used only while on qualifying active duty. Navy and Marine reserve component members can access TA only while on qualifying active duty.
RAND RR1766-A.1

We focus our attention on the two largest programs—the PGIB and TA. Next, we provide more background on each of these benefits, as well as tracing the evolution of the PGIB from 1944 to the present. Understanding this evolution is key to interpreting our results, as many of our estimates focus on changes linked to the passage of the PGIB, and thus to the expansion of benefits from the previous MGIB.

The Evolution of the GI Bill

The Original GI Bill

The original GI Bill was created to assist the large number of returning World War II veterans with their reintegration into society (Pub. L. 78-346, 1944). The benefits were earned through military service in any capacity during the war, did not need to be "selected" in any form by the veteran, and were not contingent on the veteran paying any amount into the system. The benefits consisted of both a stipend paid to the recipient and a tuition payment given directly to the educational institution. In this way, the PGIB is similar in spirit and design to the original GI Bill.

The benefits or the original bill were disbursed for attendance at any accredited university or training course, but the benefit amount was sufficient to cover attendance at the most expensive universities in the nation. Additionally, it is estimated that the benefits covered up to 50 percent of the opportunity cost of college attendance for single veterans and 75 percent of the cost for those who were married (Bound and Turner, 2002). Thus, in terms of scope and flexibility, the 1944 GI Bill was generous.[1] As we would expect, the benefit does seem to have had significant impact in increasing college attainment for white males, with the overall increase in attainment estimated to be between 32 percent and 40 percent (Bound and Turner, 2002; Stanley, 2003). This generous benefit was available to millions of veterans and likely played a significant role in shaping the middle class in the United States; for example, children of GI Bill recipients have better educational outcomes than children of similar men who did not qualify for the benefit.[2]

Over the next several decades, various educational benefit programs superseded the original GI Bill as veterans returned from conflicts in Korea and Vietnam. In general, the impact of these programs for the veteran decreased as benefit increases lagged behind increased education costs. Though increased college attainment is still observed from these programs, the estimated rate is on the lower end of the range seen from the original GI Bill (Stanley, 2003).

The Montgomery GI Bill

In 1984, Mississippi Congressman Gillespie Montgomery authored a revision to the veterans' education benefit program that would be known as the Montgomery GI Bill (MGIB). The MGIB represented a change in the concept of how benefits should be disbursed that had occurred in the decades following World War II. The scope of the MGIB was more restricted than that of previous benefit programs. There was a separate version of the program for the active and reserve components, and the percentage of the total benefit received was dependent on the length of time served. Most importantly, the MGIB required a decision on the part of the member, usually at the time of accession into the armed forces, on whether to participate and be eligible for future benefits. Selection of the program required a $100 payment by the member for the first 12 months of service, with a voluntary contribution option of up to $600 for greater future payments. Neither of these payments was refundable if the benefits were not used (Shakely, 2012).

---

[1]   See Barr (2013) for a detailed discussion of changes in educational attainment as a result of PGIB implementation.

[2]   Page, undated.

If the scope of the MGIB was restricted compared with the original GI Bill, its flexibility was greater for the recipient. Unlike the 1944 benefit package, where tuition was paid directly to the educational institution, the MGIB paid all benefits to the recipient directly. This resulted in a dual benefit for the recipient. Not only were funds received directly from the government, but those funds were typically not reported to the institution—and hence were not likely to exclude the recipient from other need-based aid available (Barr, 2013).

Though the flexibility of MGIB for the recipient may have been greater than that under previous programs, the value of the benefit itself was less. As with programs in the Korea and Vietnam eras, the amount paid to the recipient under MGIB had generally not kept pace with increased cost of education. The benefit amount was set in nominal terms by Congress and was adjusted haphazardly over time, thus resulting in unpredictable fluctuations in the value of the benefit to the recipient (Simon, Negrusa, and Warner, 2010). This lack of value became more visible and concerning to lawmakers as U.S. military operations increased following the 9/11 attacks. By 2005, VA officials were warning that enlistees should not join the armed forces for education benefits alone—the benefits would increasingly lag behind education costs (Farrell, 2005). Fearful of recruiting shortfalls and under pressure from veterans groups, Congress began considering an overhaul of the veterans' education benefit system in 2007.

Chapter 33—The Post-9/11 GI Bill

Fiscal year 2005 saw significant shortfalls in recruiting across the board, but particularly in the Army and Marine Corps. The general belief among DoD officials was that the recruitment gap was due to the worsening situation in the conflicts overseas, particularly in Iraq (Cordesman and Sullivan, 2006). Interest groups such as the Iraq and Afghanistan Veterans of America (IAVA) lobbied extensively for a revision to education benefits that they believed would reverse the negative recruiting trend. Despite broad support for military assistance programs, some opposed a revision to the MGIB based on the belief that an overly generous benefit package would lower reenlistment probability (Williamson, 2008).

In February 2008, Sen. Jim Webb (D-Va.) introduced the "Post-9/11 Veterans Educational Assistance Act of 2008," known also as Chapter 33. The bill sought to establish an educational assistance program rivaling the original World War II-era package. The proposed assistance program did not permit attendance at *any* campus desired, but it did represent a substantial increase in benefits for most veterans.

The increase in benefits is not automatic for all recipients. The 2008 benefit was originally more restrictive on the types of education that made one eligible. Additionally, the 2008 benefit was paid directly to the institution, with the student receiving a living allowance based on the housing allowance paid to an E-5 with dependents in that locality. This part of the benefit varied greatly, from $801 in Ohio to $2,701 in New York City (Steele, Salcedo, and Coley, 2011). Therefore, a student attending a school where the tuition and fees are waived for veterans and who would receive a housing benefit less than the MGIB level of $1,426 per month might have no incentive to choose the Chapter 33 benefits. Thus, the Chapter 33 benefits did not take the place of the MGIB, but rather were a separate option. However, if a student is eligible for both types of assistance based on MGIB contributions, he or she must make an irrevocable choice when applying for the benefit. The exception to this stipulation is that students eligible for both who have exhausted their MGIB benefits can receive 12 months of Chapter 33 benefits (Martorell and Bergman, 2013).

The Chapter 33 benefits also included an option not seen in previous veterans' education assistance programs. Service members meeting certain criteria for time in service and time remaining are able to transfer their benefits to their dependents. In addition to making the benefit more expansive, the transferability also addresses long-standing concerns that education benefits negatively impact retention in the armed forces.

In 2010, Congress passed a modification to the Chapter 33 assistance program, commonly referred to as GI Bill 2.0. In addition to expanded coverage of nondegree programs, the new bill also established a national cap of $17,500 for tuition and fees. This calculation would now be based on the student's total aid package—the expectation being that colleges would allocate aid dollars to nonveterans and veterans would be discouraged from applying for other scholarships (American Council on Education, 2011). In addition to these changes, the tuition rate was no longer pegged to the in-state tuition of that state's most expensive public university. Instead, the 2010 version tied assistance to the in-state tuition of the institution the recipient actually attended (Martorell and Bergman, 2013). The difference was substantial in several states.

Key Differences in Post-9/11 GI Bill Benefits

The PGIB (to include the revisions instituted in 2010) represented several changes in both scope and flexibility for recipients over the MGIB. The scope was significantly increased in terms of eligible participation and applicability for educational programs. Eligibility for the benefit under the new program was based on aggregate time in service, with no deliberate decision on the part of the member required. This is in contrast to the MGIB, under which eligibility was determined by a decision made by the member, usually at the time of accession. Additionally, the time that a recipient is given to use the benefit was increased to 15 years, a five-year increase over the eligibility for the MGIB (VA, 2014; VA, 2011).

Finally, recipients may be eligible to transfer their benefits to their dependents if they meet certain requirements of time in service and obligated time remaining. DoD approves requests to transfer all or the unused portion of education benefits from the service member to a dependent enrolled in the Defense Enrollment Eligibility Reporting System (DEERS). In addition to being of benefit to military families, this new facet of VA educational assistance may address concerns about a negative impact on retention. Service members are required to have a combination of performed and obligated service that ensures their service goes beyond the minimum requirement for joining (VA, 2013). In fact, before the Post-9/11 GI Bill was enacted in August 2009, some DoD policymakers were concerned that the relative increase in benefit generosity of Chapter 33 compared with Chapter 30 (MGIB) could have negative implications for retention.[3] The benefit transfer option was, in part, a response to this concern.

The change in flexibility of benefits brought about by the Chapter 33 legislation is more difficult to determine. The PGIB tuition payments are in-kind benefits, paid directly to the institution and thus not available for any use the recipient sees fit. This lack of choice for the recipient could be interpreted as reducing the flexibility of the benefit. But using data from the 2010 National Survey of Veterans, Barr (2015) has shown that two flexibility-enhancing aspects of the Chapter 33 benefits outweigh the loss of the cash transfer to the student.

First, the inability to keep unused funds from the tuition benefit has led recipients to choose more expensive institutions than those chosen under the MGIB (Barr, 2015). Under MGIB, the student had an incentive to choose an educational program with cost below that of the monthly benefit. The Chapter 33 benefits are pegged to actual costs of schools in the recipient's state and, therefore, remove that incentive. Thus recipients are incentivized to pick a more expensive program if appropriate and covered under the benefit cap. The second aspect of the Post-9/11 GI Bill that provides flexibility is the geographic variance in benefits. The standard benefit under MGIB encouraged attendance at the least expensive school in an area with low cost of living. Under Chapter 33, recipients are paid a living allowance roughly equal to that of an E-5 for their locality. As previously discussed, this benefit ranged from $800 to $2,700 and made selection of an institution in a more expensive area more viable than it would have been under the flat-rate benefit MGIB program.

Surveys of veterans indicate that the recipients consider the Chapter 33 benefits more flexible and that their choices are now based on the best education option rather than the best financial option. Steele, Salcedo, and Coley (2011) conducted focus groups of veterans enrolled in educational programs and found that the housing allowance with geographic variance is one of the most popular facets of the new benefit program. A second positive element of the Chapter 33 legislation was identified as the ability to keep MGIB benefits if the service member is eligible and decides they are a better option for the circumstances. This also adds to the flexibility of the Chapter 33 program, since many veterans had already paid into the MGIB program and might get greater benefit from the cash transfer (Martorell and Bergman, 2013).

---

[3]   Based on discussions with DoD accession policy staff, June 2016.

As of late 2015, when our PGIB file was collected, the PGIB had been used by over 1.2 million service members, at a total cost of over $39 billion.[4] Over 450,000 service members had transferred at least some portion of their PGIB benefit to a spouse and/or to one or more children; transferring only to children is the most common pattern. As of late 2015, at least some transferred benefits had been used by nearly 250,000 dependents (spouses or children of service members).

Tuition Assistance

The various versions of the GI Bill and Veterans Education Assistance Program were not the only programs instituted to assist service members with meeting their education goals. TA is another key education benefit. Each service has a TA program for current service members to pursue education at civilian institutions while they are on active duty. The programs are administered separately for each service, with each having slightly different requirements. After the TA programs were established, Congress mandated that they provide a uniform level of benefits between them. This fixed amount of support for education in off-duty time had effects that may be relevant when considering GI Bill impacts.

TA is a widely used benefit; service members enrolled in over 9 million courses during the time period included in our data (FY 2003–FY 2015). The total amount spent on TA over this time period was roughly $5 billion. The number of courses varied by year, from roughly 500,000 to 900,000 (including enrollments by active component and reserve component personnel in the Army, Navy, Air Force, and Marine Corps); yearly costs averaged about $380 million. The overall usage of the benefit fell during the period covered by our data.

---

[4] PGIB spending is reported in nominal dollars, not adjusted for inflation. Because the PGIB files do not indicate the date of each payment, it is not possible to adjust these figures to account for inflation since the program began.

Additional Data on TA and PGIB

Our data on usage of TA provided more detail than our data on PGIB usage. Here, we present additional, detailed TA-specific results. The information on service members and their career progression is derived from several files provided by DMDC; these are the same files used to produce the results in Chapter Five. The TA data include course-level observations on all courses that utilized TA funds, across a number of years (FY 2003–FY 2015).[1] We were able to link these data to our information on service members.[2]

While our data include the name of each course, there is no standard code indicating the course's subject or level. Therefore, it is not possible to accurately categorize the level of courses taken. However, we were able to shorten and standardize the course names somewhat; Figure B.1 presents a word cloud made up of names that appear in course titles. The relative size of the word indicates the frequency with which it appears. This figure clearly indicates that, while service members use TA to take courses in a very wide range of subjects, it appears that many service members take introductory courses that are at least somewhat general in nature.

As a second method of characterizing courses, we also sorted on course name and calculated the most common course titles; the list includes the following courses:

- College Algebra
- English Composition (I and II)
- Introduction to/General Psychology
- Foundations of Online Learning
- Public Speaking
- Intermediate Algebra
- Introduction to Sociology.

---

[1] We would like to express our appreciation to the service representatives who provided the data, as well as to Dawn Bilodeau and Jonathan Woods of the DoD Voluntary Education Office for their assistance in obtaining these data.

[2] We are grateful to Scott Seggerman of DMDC, for assisting with the data coordination and match.

Figure B.1
Word Cloud Based on Tuition Assistance Course Titles

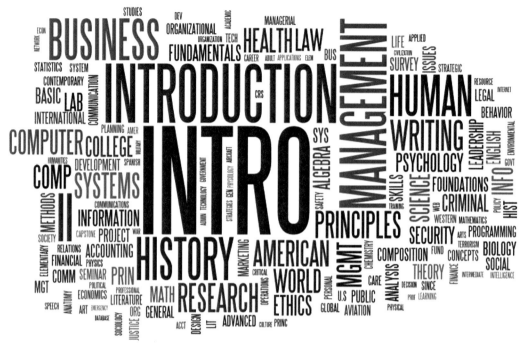

SOURCE: RAND NDRI analysis of random 10-percent subsample of TA course titles, FY 2003–FY 2015, using wordle.com.
RAND *RR1766-B.1*

These courses are fairly general in nature, are likely to be prerequisites for more advanced coursework, and are likely to add to general knowledge (or general "human capital") as opposed to focusing on knowledge directly required for service members' current jobs.

Postsecondary Institutions Receiving TA Funds

Our data include observations on over 1 million unique service members; these service members attended nearly 4,700 unique postsecondary institutions.[3] However, a few institutions offer the vast majority of TA courses; we find that 97 percent of all courses are offered by 10 percent of institutions (466 institutions), and fully 40 percent of the courses are offered by only 10 institutions. Funds are concentrated in a similar manner.

The data include the name of the institution and an identification number. Based on this information, we were able to match ED data on institutional characteristics and

---

[3]   This is likely an undercount; about 10 percent of observations lack an institution identification number.

weight the institution characteristics by the incidence of usage by different user groups so as to reflect the average institution characteristics for members of four user groups: (1) service members using TA;[4] (2) service members using PGIB;[5] (3) dependents using PGIB;[6] and (4) the general population of U.S. college students.[7] These data reveal that the institutions offering TA might be considered less "selective" than others, based on admittance rate and average SAT of attendees, but the graduates of these institutions actually earn more than typical graduates (see Table B.1).[8]

Educational Milestones: Credits Earned, Estimated Cost per Credit

As noted in the main body of this report, the TA benefit includes several limits; courses generally are reimbursed so long as the cost remains at or below $250 per credit hour ($750 for a typical course), and service members may use up to $4,500 in TA benefits per (fiscal) year. In most cases, service members do not hit the maximum yearly benefit, perhaps because they take courses in concert with full-time employment. Also, TA does not provide any allowance for living expenses. The limits of per-course and total spending, and the lack of other allowances, suggest that TA should be far less costly than PGIB. And indeed, we find that to be the case. Our data on TA spending spans about 13 years; over that time period, the total spending was roughly $5 billion on somewhat more than 1 million service members. The PGIB, in contrast, had been in

Table B.1
Characteristics of Schools Receiving TA Funds

User Group	Admin Rate (%)	Average SAT	Pell Eligible (%)	Median Earnings ($)
Members using TA	86.4	1026	31.9	42,130
Members using PGIB	66.3	1077	40.7	35,581
Dependents using PGIB	66.2	1088	37.6	36,420
General student population	63.6	1111	38.1	35,886

NOTE: Institutional characteristics and outcomes from the Integrated Postsecondary Education Database (IPEDS) and the College Scorecard weighted by usage patterns for different user groups.

---

[4]   Weighted by number of TA courses delivered at the institution.

[5]   Weighted by number of months of PGIB benefit used by service member beneficiaries at the institution.

[6]   Weighted by number of months of PGIB benefit used by dependent beneficiaries at the institution.

[7]   Weighted by full-time equivalent enrollment at the institution.

[8]   Given the heavy concentration of service members in some schools, eventual salaries of service members could play some role in these figures.

existence for about seven years when our data were collected; at that point, total spending (for about 1.2 million current or former service members) was in the neighborhood of $40 billion. As of late 2015, total spending on the 250,000 dependents who had used the benefit was roughly $8 billion.

The PGIB is far more expensive in terms of total spending, and in terms of spending per service member, than TA, but service members using TA typically complete few courses. The majority of TA users complete less than 15 hours (roughly one semester) of credits; the vast majority complete less than 30 hours (two semesters) of credits. Even a few credits may be helpful to service members preparing to use the PGIB; while the PGIB provides a total of 36 months of benefits, typical time to degree among those attending four-year colleges has increased sharply in recent years (see, e.g., Cataldi et al., 2011). Therefore, beginning college with some credits acquired through TA may be one key to on-time graduation. Also, completing even a few courses may assist service members in deciding whether they would like to attend college and what they would like to study, while also adding to their general human capital and skills in the interim.

Cost per Semester, PGIB and TA

As discussed in the main text, the PGIB data do not include information on the number of courses or credits completed. Indeed, the files do not even include definitive indications of start and stop dates. However, the files do indicate the total spending per service member on the living allowance, as well as the current monthly amount of the living allowance. From these variables, it is possible to form a rough estimate of the number of months of benefits used. We use this to estimate the overall cost per semester (assuming four months of benefits equates to 1 semester).[9] We can compare this cost to the cost of a semester of credits obtained through TA.

The results of these rough estimates indicate that the cost of one semester of credits through TA is about $3,000 (about $600 per course). For service members, we estimate the PGIB costs are roughly $4,100 per semester in tuition and fees, or $9,300 per semester in total costs. For dependents, the PGIB costs are roughly $4,400 per semester in tuition and fees, or $9,400 per semester in total costs. Therefore, while the PGIB is much more expensive than TA in total, the tuition and fees costs per semester of credit are more comparable (in this case, PGIB exceeds TA by about 35 percent).

The PGIB is designed for full-time use, and thus should result in the service member earning credits far more quickly than with TA. Indeed, our estimates indicate that this is the case. We estimate that those using the PGIB have earned some 5

---

[9]   Of course, this calculation involves significant caveats—in particular, it is likely to be inaccurate in cases when students switch schools, fail courses, attend on a part-time basis, etc. In such cases, we are likely to overestimate the semesters of credit and underestimate the cost per semester.

million semesters of credits (again, assuming that four months of benefits equates to a semester of credit). Those using TA earned about 1.6 million semesters of credits, even though we have considerably more years of TA data. These calculations also reveal that one reason PGIB spending on dependents exceeds that on service members is that dependents who have begun to use the benefit have used slightly more months on average than service members.[10] In summary, PGIB is more costly than TA. However, the difference per estimated semester of credit is much smaller than the difference in total spending or in spending per service member because those using PGIB appear to complete substantially more coursework than the typical service member using TA.

---

[10] As discussed earlier, dependents attend more expensive schools, and that explains part of the difference as well. However, dependents have attended those schools for a slightly longer period than service members, thus presumably earning more credits. This explains why the cost per semester between dependents and service members differs somewhat less than might be expected based solely on Figure 5.1.

Additional Quantitative Results

In this appendix, we include a table of descriptive statistics, as well as a variety of additional quantitative results. Many are the result of specification tests, or of analyses by service.

Table C.1
Summary Statistics for Accession Characteristics, Enlisted Service Members, Active Component

		Army	Air Force	Marines	Navy	All Services
High AFQT	Mean	0.638	0.846	0.695	0.744	0.711
	Std. Dev.	0.481	0.361	0.461	0.437	0.453
Age	Mean	21.191	20.264	19.498	20.515	20.540
	Std. Dev.	3.669	2.296	1.940	2.920	3.058
Female	Mean	0.161	0.211	0.074	0.190	0.160
	Std. Dev.	0.368	0.408	0.262	0.393	0.367
Has. Dep.	Mean	0.190	0.124	0.039	0.101	0.129
	Std. Dev.	0.392	0.330	0.194	0.301	0.335
Race: Asian	Mean	0.165	0.039	0.038	0.060	0.094
	Std. Dev.	0.371	0.193	0.192	0.238	0.291
Race: Black	Mean	0.172	0.156	0.089	0.170	0.153
	Std. Dev.	0.378	0.363	0.285	0.376	0.360
Race: Hispanic	Mean	0.116	0.013	0.112	0.115	0.096
	Std. Dev.	0.320	0.111	0.316	0.319	0.294
Race: Other	Mean	0.022	0.041	0.018	0.127	0.049
	Std. Dev.	0.146	0.198	0.133	0.333	0.215
Some College	Mean	0.129	0.106	0.034	0.078	0.095
	Std. Dev.	0.335	0.308	0.182	0.268	0.293
BA/BS Degree	Mean	0.019	0.035	0.007	0.008	0.017
	Std. Dev.	0.135	0.185	0.085	0.087	0.129
Total Count		803,459	10376,013	391,092	462,175	2,032,739

Table C.2
Enlistment Quality Hypothesis 1 Regression Results: Change in Cohort Quality Post-PGIB (by service, coefficient on post-PGIB reported)

		Army	Navy	Marines	Air Force
Active	Mean AFQT	1.559***	0.255	−0.222	0.429
		(0.331)	(0.377)	(0.421)	(0.321)
	Prop. High AFQT	0.0295***	−0.0122	−0.00798	0.0141
		(0.00807)	(0.00866)	(0.00982)	(0.00743)
Reserves	Mean AFQT	3.199***	−0.291	−2.588**	−3.094
		(0.320)	(0.910)	(0.789)	(4.275)
	Prop. High AFQT	0.0965***	−0.00997	−0.0128	0.112
		(0.00840)	(0.0229)	(0.0202)	(0.106)

NOTES: ***$p < 0.01$, **$p < 0.05$, *$p < 0.1$, adjusted for multiple hypotheses.

Standard errors in parentheses. Control variables: state unemployment rate, service authorized strength, quadratic in year, fraction each race, fraction female, state dummies.

Table C.3
Retention Hypothesis 1, National Interrupted Time-Series Regression Results: Change in Continuation Rates Post-PGIB (by service)

		Past 5	Past 6	Past 7
Active	Army	−0.0348***	−0.0284***	−0.0280***
		(0.00262)	(0.00290)	(0.00315)
	Navy	−0.0125***	−0.0264***	−0.0244***
		(0.00348)	(0.00381)	(0.00408)
	Marines	−0.0254***	−0.0232***	−0.0290***
		(0.00375)	(0.00380)	(0.00401)
	Air Force	−0.0116***	−0.0212***	−0.0187***
		(0.00337)	(0.00405)	(0.00441)
Reserves	Army	−0.00876***	−0.0259***	−0.0145***
		(0.00238)	(0.00329)	(0.00365)
	Navy	−0.0582***	−0.0545***	−0.0260
		(0.0137)	(0.0153)	(0.0163)
	Marines	0.0148	0.000274	−0.0127
		(0.00640)	(0.00902)	(0.00892)
	Air Force	0.0650***	0.0331	0.0254
		(0.0176)	(0.0235)	(0.0269)

NOTES: ***$p < 0.01$, **$p < 0.05$, *$p < 0.1$, adjusted for multiple hypotheses.

Standard errors in parentheses. Control variables: having dependents, gender, race dummies, cumulative completed courses, high AFQT score, college attainment, age, months deployed in past six months, resident state unemployment rate, service authorized strength, quadratic in years, skill level, month dummies, state dummies, pay status dummies, MOS dummies, service dummies.

Table C.4
Retention Hypothesis 2, National Difference-in-Differences Regression Results: Differential Change in Continuation Rates Post-PGIB for Those with Dependents (by service)

		Past 5	Past 6	Past 7
Active	Army	0.0303***	0.0229***	0.00838**
		(0.00176)	(0.00206)	(0.00239)
	Navy	0.00545	0.0141***	0.0244***
		(0.00225)	(0.00262)	(0.00305)
	Marines	0.00527	−0.000581	0.00196
		(0.00239)	(0.00241)	(0.00299)
	Air Force	0.00328	0.0133***	0.0187***
		(0.00212)	(0.00271)	(0.00318)
Reserve	Army	0.0126***	0.0191***	0.0185***
		(0.00168)	(0.00243)	(0.00288)
	Navy	−0.0245	−0.000752	−0.00439
		(0.00942)	(0.0108)	(0.0126)
	Marines	0.00781	0.0122	0.0252*
		(0.00546)	(0.00808)	(0.00843)
	Air Force	0.0140	0.0306	0.00211
		(0.0112)	(0.0159)	(0.0193)

NOTES: ***$p < 0.01$, **$p < 0.05$, *$p < 0.1$, adjusted for multiple hypotheses.

STANDARD errors in parentheses. Control variables: having dependents, gender, race dummies, cumulative completed courses, high AFQT score, college attainment, age, months deployed in past six months, resident state unemployment rate, service authorized strength, quadratic in years, skill level, month dummies, state dummies, pay status dummies, MOS dummies, service dummies.

Table C.5
In-Service Hypothesis 1, National Interrupted Time-Series Regressions, Change in TA Usage from Passage of PGIB (by service)

	Active		Reserves	
	Cross-Sectional	Fixed Effects	Cross-Sectional	Fixed Effects
Army	0.0974***	0.0981**	−0.0957	−0.106
	(0.0272)	(0.0314)	(0.0909)	(0.112)
Navy	0.191***	0.316***	0.109	0.252**
	(0.0186)	(0.0235)	(0.0718)	(0.0899)
Marines	0.0716***	0.0881**	0.166	0.127
	(0.0208)	(0.0284)	(0.129)	(0.19)
Air Force	0.0634***	0.113***	−0.399**	0.302
	(0.0143)	(0.0163)	(0.142)	(0.258)

NOTES: ***$p < 0.01$, **$p < .005$, *$p < 0.1$, adjusted for multiple hypotheses.
Standard errors in parentheses
Control variables: total previously completed TA courses, years of service, having dependents, gender, race dummies, cumulative completed courses, high AFQT score, college attainment, age, months deployed in past six months, resident state unemployment rate, service authorized strength, quadratic in years, skill level, month dummies, state dummies, pay status dummies, MOS dummies, service dummies.

Table C.6
In-Service Hypothesis 1, National Interrupted Time-Series Regressions, Change in TA Usage for Each Additional Prior Completed TA Course (by service)

	Active		Reserves	
	Cross-Sectional	Fixed Effects	Cross-Sectional	Fixed Effects
Army	0.0352***	−0.0502***	0.0194***	−0.107***
	(0.000685)	(0.00116)	(0.00202)	(0.00408)
Navy	0.0611***	−0.0609***	0.0294***	−0.0826***
	(0.000543)	(0.00105)	(0.00187)	(0.00407)
Marines	0.0560***	−0.0876***	0.0244***	−0.119***
	(0.000681)	(0.00132)	(0.00328)	(0.00956)
Air Force	0.0557***	−0.0660***	0.0385***	−0.0962***
	(0.000315)	(0.000592)	(0.00246)	(0.0103)

NOTES: ***$p < 0.01$, **$p < 0.05$, *$p < 0.1$, adjusted for multiple hypotheses.
Standard errors in parentheses. Control variables: post-PGIB, years of service, having dependents, gender, race dummies, cumulative completed courses, high AFQT score, college attainment, age, months deployed in past six months, resident state unemployment rate, service authorized strength, quadratic in years, skill level, month dummies, state dummies, pay status dummies, MOS dummies, service dummies.

Table C.7
In-Service Hypothesis 2: Difference-in-Differences Regressions, Differential Change in TA Usage from Passage of PGIB for Those with Dependents (by service)

	Active		Reserves	
	Cross-Sectional	Fixed Effects	Cross-Sectional	Fixed Effects
Army	−0.0123	−0.000856	0.123	0.198
	(0.0211)	(0.0281)	(0.0664)	(0.0980)
Navy	−0.0535***	−0.00638	0.00959	0.00856
	(0.0121)	(0.0199)	(0.0466)	(0.0754)
Marines	−0.115***	−0.107***	−0.0882	−0.0941
	(0.0134)	(0.0243)	(0.0953)	(0.192)
Air Force	0.0205	0.00105	0.0976	0.0861
	(0.00927)	(0.0135)	(0.103)	(0.274)

NOTES: ***$p < 0.01$, **$p < 0.05$, *$p < 0.1$, adjusted for multiple hypotheses.

Standard errors in parentheses. Control variables: post-PGIB, years of service, having dependents, gender, race dummies, cumulative completed courses, high AFQT score, college attainment, age, months deployed in past six months, resident state unemployment rate, service authorized strength, quadratic in years, skill level, month dummies, state dummies, pay status dummies, MOS dummies, service dummies.

Table C.8
In-Service Hypothesis 3: Regression Results, Effect of TA and PGIB Usage on Promotion Tempo (by service)

		TA	PGIB
Promote to E5 at 3 Years	Army	8.46e-05	−0.000347**
		(0.000283)	(0.000129)
	Navy	0.0356***	0.00998***
		(0.00122)	(0.000941)
	Marines	0.0387***	0.00757***
		(0.00122)	(0.000941)
	Air Force	−0.000335	−0.000265
		(0.000242)	(0.000238)
Promote to E5 at 4 Years	Army	0.00128***	0.000577***
		(0.000366)	(0.000173)
	Navy	0.0630***	0.0160***
		(0.00326)	(0.00270)
	Marines	0.114***	0.0420***
		(0.00326)	(0.00270)
	Air Force	0.0491***	0.00835**
		(0.00268)	(0.00272)

NOTES: TA: Regression coefficients on having taken TA during service. PGIB: Regression coefficient post-service on taking up PGIB.
$***p < 0.01$, $**p < 0.05$, $*p < 0.1$, adjusted for multiple hypotheses. Standard errors in parentheses. Control variables: post-PGIB, years of service, having dependents, gender, race dummies, cumulative completed courses, high AFQT score, college attainment, age, months deployed in past six months, resident state unemployment rate, service authorized strength, quadratic in years, skill level, month dummies, state dummies, pay status dummies, MOS dummies, service dummies.

Table C.9
In-Service Hypotheses 4: Regression Results, Effect of TA Usage on PGIB Take-Up (by service)

Army	Navy	Marines	Air Force
0.0102***	0.00970***	0.0134***	0.00813***
(0.000305)	(0.000317)	(0.000333)	(0.000227)

NOTES: $***p < 0.01$, $**p < 0.05$, $*p < 0.1$, adjusted for multiple hypotheses.
Standard errors in parentheses. Control variables: years of service, having dependents, gender, race dummies, cumulative completed courses, high AFQT score, college attainment, age, months deployed in past six months, resident state unemployment rate, service authorized strength, quadratic in years, skill level, month dummies, state dummies, pay status dummies, MOS dummies, service dummies.

Additional Information on Internet Search Data

The types of search query analyses possible depend in large part on the structure of the available data. In this report, we use search volume data gathered from Google Trends and Google AdWords' Keyword Planner. The data provided by each tool differs, making each better suited for exploring certain questions. Table D.1 highlights some of the similarities and differences between the tools.

Table D.1
Comparison of Google Trends and Google AdWords

	Google Trends	Google AdWords
Usage	Compares search term(s) across time and location. Suggests related popular searches (broad match).	Absolute volume of search term across time and location. Suggests related popular searches (exact match).
Time period	2004–present	2 years
Frequency	Weekly (default), minute-by-minute possible	Monthly
Search type	Broad	Exact
Search units	Relative to peak value	Absolute number
Geographic filters	Country / state / metro / city	Up to 10 locations, as fine as postal code level
Side-by-side comparison	Up to 5 queries (any search term)	n/a
Negative keywords	X	X
Additional filters	Web, image, YouTube, news, and shopping	Computer, mobile, and tablet

There are two major differences between Google Trends and Google AdWords. First, Google Trends furnishes search query data based on the *relative* search volume (values range from 0 to 100), in relation to the peak search volume for that term during a specified time, or the peak search volume across all terms when multiple keywords are being evaluated.[1] The location of search can be specified using filters, to separate searches by country, state, or even city. It is also possible to filter results by date: Weekly search results are available from 2004 onward, daily search results are available for the past 90 days, hourly search results are available for the past seven days, and minute-by-minute search results are available for the past day. In concert with these features, category filters can be used to return only those results that Google has identified as falling into a specified category.[2] In contrast, the Google AdWords tool reports data based on the *absolute* number of searches for each term. In that sense, Google AdWords is more precise. However, data for Google AdWords are available for a maximum of only two years, whereas data for Google Trends is available from 2004.

The second major difference between the tools is that Google Trends reports data on *broad* matches of search terms, whereas Google AdWords reports data on *exact* matches. For example, a query on Google Trends for the term "education" will include searches that include keywords such as "degree" or "school." This is useful for general searches, where there is interest in learning about a keyword category without wishing to identify and assemble the exhaustive list of potential queries. Google AdWords, on the other hand, will return the search frequency for only queries that contain the exact term, such as "higher education" or "jobs in education." This is helpful when trying to learn about a very precise query, such as "VA education benefits." To summarize, Google Trends reports relative search volume, on a broadly matched set of terms, from 2004 forward; Google AdWords, in contrast, reports the absolute number of searches, based on exact matches, from the previous two years.

We use Google Trends and Google AdWords in tandem; this allows us to utilize the strengths of each tool when conducting our analysis. For uncovering people's general attitudes toward the military, and for tracking general education-related searches across time and space, we use data from Google Trends. (It is also possible to use Google Trends when examining the time of day for which searches are conducted, due mainly to a new feature that allows data to be requested at the minute-by-minute level.) We rely on data from Google AdWords to collect information on the most popular

---

[1]   Therefore, it is not possible to see the absolute number of searches using Google Trends, although it is possible to compare results from different terms to discern which is the more prevalent.

[2]   The broad categories available to choose from are Arts & Entertainment, Autos & Vehicles, Beauty & Fitness, Books & Literature, Business & Industrial, Computers & Electronics, Finance, Food & Drink, Games, Health, Hobbies & Leisure, Home & Garden, Internet & Telecom, Jobs & Education, Law & Government, News, Online Communities, People & Society, Pets & Animals, Real Estate, Reference, Science, Shopping, Sports, Travel. It should be noted that the method by which Google assigns a search into a given category is not transparent, though past research suggests it is likely to be accurate (Jahedi, Wenger, and Yeung, 2016).

questions posed on a specific topic, such as a branch of the military, or an educational benefit, such as the PGIB. In such cases, we include searches for "army," "navy," "air force," "marines," and "military" to avoid unwanted inclusions,[3] and the results were filtered by the Google-assigned category "Law & Government" with a second filter for the subcategory "Military." Thus, the reported results are for only those searches that Google has determined are military-related.

Both the search data and the applicant data are aggregated at the monthly level from January 2004 through August 2015 (Google analytics data are not available prior to January 2004). Of course, it is possible that search terms do not happen in the same month as applications; for this reason, we also test the inclusion of a one-month lagged term for each query. The lagged queries turn out to matter only for the term ASVAB, so we do not include the other lagged queries. The search frequency of the term ASVAB, when included in our regressions without other search terms, is highly predictive of changes in the high-quality applications for each branch of the military. The coefficient ranges from 6.8 percent (Marines) to 10.2 percent (Air Force). Note that the R-squared measures in these simple models are roughly 0.8, meaning that much of the variance in applications is explained. This does not appear to be completely driven by the month and year indicators; removing those variables from our model returns an R-squared of about 0.6.

The term "[service] jobs" is also, without other search terms, quite a good predictor of applicants in all branches with the exception of the Marines. In the cases of the Navy and the Air Force, the coefficient is 4.6 percent and 6.3 percent, respectively. For the Army, the coefficient is nearly 10 percent, meaning that it is comparable in size to searches related to ASVAB. We also experimented with the more general terms "join [service]" and "[service] salary," which turned out to be significant only in the case of the Air Force.[4]

We expect search behavior across similar terms to be correlated—in other words, when more people search about information related to joining a service, they likely also search for information related to salary. Therefore, we next included all of the search terms in a single regression. (See Table D.2.) Consistent with our hypothesis of correlation, fewer search terms are now statistically significant (in a regression equation, such correlation among explanatory variables is referred to as *multicollinearity*). However, in each case the current or lagged searches on ASVAB are still statistically significant. The effect sizes are substantive, with the exception of the Army (a 10-percent increase in service-specific ASVAB searches is now correlated with a 6- to 7-percent increase in high-quality applicants for the Navy and the Marine Corps). In the case of the Army, job-related searches remain important; in the case of the Air Force, salary-related

---

[3]   This is to ensure that unrelated terms, such as "swiss army knives" or "navy blue jeans," are precluded from the analysis.

[4]   We tried variants of this term, such as "[Service] pay" to see if the phrasing made a difference but in all situations, searches for pay-related terms only explain high quality applications to the Air Force.

Table D.2
Predicting Service Applications by Using Multiple Search Terms

	Army	Navy	AirForce	Marines
	All	All	All	All
ASVAB	0.005	0.072**	0.039	0.062**
	[0.038]	[0.030]	[0.032]	[0.027]
ASVB (lagged)	0.007**	0.003	0.009***	0.003
	[0.003]	[0.003]	[0.003]	[0.003]
[Service] jobs	0.079***	0.012	0.012	−0.026
	[0.030]	[0.024]	[0.025]	[0.017]
[Service] salary	−0.006	−0.016	0.078***	0.012
	[0.024]	[0.030]	[0.023]	[0.019]
Join [service]	−0.012	0.006	0.005	0
	[0.031]	[0.021]	[0.021]	[0.020]
Month-fixed effect	X	X	X	X
Year-fixed effect	X	X	X	X
Constant	8.053***	7.661***	7.084***	7.476***
	[0.141]	[0.132]	[0.154]	[0.124]
R-squared	0.828	0.838	0.852	0.787
Observations	139	139	139	139

SOURCE: RAND NRDI analysis, based on Google Trends data and on Applicant data.

NOTE: Data are at the monthly level, from January 2004 to August 2015. ** indicates statistical significance at the 5-percent level or better. *** indicates statistical significance at the 1-percent level or better.

searches remain important. In each of these cases, the effect sizes are approximately the same as the ASVAB effect sizes for the Navy and Marine Corps. In summary, service-specific searches are correlated with high-quality applicants, but our data suggest that interest in different searches may be seeking somewhat different types of information.

Table D.2 includes regression results of applicants based on month and year fixed effects, as well as a series of Google search terms. Specifically, we include the relative intensity of search for each of these terms. Our data are at the monthly level and span the period January 2004 to August 2015 (Google analytics data are not available prior to January 2004). Standard errors appear below each estimated coefficient in square brackets. The dependent variable is the log of the number of high-quality applicants, where high-quality applicants are defined as those who hold a high school diploma or equivalent and scored at least 50 on the AFQT.

Status of Forces Analyses, Methods, and Data Description

For this analysis, we used the Status of Forces (SOF) Survey of Active Duty Members, years 2002–2013. The SOF survey is a randomly sampled web-based survey. Each year, the SOF takes randomly selected cross-sectional samples of active-duty members, reserve members, and DoD civilian employees (we use only the surveys of active-duty members for our analyses). Since 2002, this survey has been conducted between one and four times per year where the population of interest is all active-duty members of the Army, Navy, Marine Corps, and Air Force, up to and including pay grade O-6, with a minimum of six months of service. The data used for this analysis include 27 waves and close to 350,000 observations.

Methods

The SOF survey sampling frame was created by stratifying on six variables including service type, gender, pay grade, race/ethnicity, region, and family. To choose the number of individuals sampled for each stratum, the survey designers used a sample planning tool developed for the DMDC (2013), which utilizes Karush-Kuhn-Tucker theory (Chromy, 1987). The procedure is designed to deliver precision constraints (e.g., ± 5 percent) on prevalence estimates for the principle reporting domains. The survey dates ranged from 2002 to 2012; the survey questions of interest were administered three times per year in 2003–2009, once in 2010, once in 2011, and twice in 2012. We also used the first survey from 2013.

All analyses were performed using Statistical Analysis System version 9.3 and employed a two-tailed type 1 error of 0.05 as the threshold for statistical significance. P-values for type 3 tests are also included for each model, presented in the footnotes of each plot. These will indicate if there is a statistically significant difference in proportions between: groups within each stratum, trend (overall proportions over time), and interaction (if the trend over time differs between the subgroups).

Analyses

Variables of interest available in more than one survey year were analyzed over time in a repeat cross-sectional framework, stratified by our four factor variables of interest (pay grade, dependents, years of service, education). An overall time trend was also included in each plot for comparison. The proportion of individuals responding with agreement, along with a 95-percent confidence interval, was calculated from a survey weighted logistic regression for each variable. The regression models included the factor variable of interest, a time trend, and a time by factor interaction; the model was estimated using a Taylor series method (recommended by the survey designers). This specification allows us to demonstrate differences between subgroup levels (e.g., dependents versus no dependents), trends in time, and a difference in differences, i.e., changes in the differences between factor levels over time.

We stratify the data into the following subgroups:

- Years of service: less than 3, 3 to less than 6, 6 to less than 10, 10 or more
- Pay grade: E-1 to E-4, E-5 to E-9, W-1 to W-5, O-1 to O-3, O-4 to O-6.
- Dependents: Has dependents, does not have dependents.
- Service members' level of education: high school or less, some college, college degree or more.

Descriptive Statistics

Close to 40 percent of the sample was made up of individuals with an E-5–E-9 pay grade; the majority had been deployed since 9/11, and there was a fairly even distribution between service branches. The majority of respondents were white, male, and had dependents. More than half were deployed in the past year, and about 45 percent had ten or more years of service. These statistics suggest that the sample was only somewhat reflective of the entire active component. However, we weighted our analyses so that the sample is reflective of the active component in terms of measurable characteristics. Table E.1 lists each variable used, and the surveys in which that variable was included.

The majority of the survey responses used a Likert scale. In the survey, Likert scale variables range from 1 to 5, where 1 is associated with a "strongly disagree" response and 5 is associated with "strongly agree" (though the survey uses different wording in some cases to elucidate "agreement").[1] For ease of analysis and interpretation, we

---

[1]   Depending on the question, the exact wording of the response varied; examples of wording used include the following: how satisfied (very dissatisfied to very satisfied); how important (not important to very important); to what extent were/was . . . (not at all to very large extent); how did X affect . . . (greatly decreased to greatly increased); how likely are you to . . . (very unlikely to very likely); how much did the following contribute to . .

Table E.1
Education Benefit–Related Variables Included in Analysis

Variable Name		
Strata Variables	**Description**	**Available in Surveys**
YrsofServ	Years of Service (<3, 3–6, 6–10,10+ years)	02/07, 03/03, 04/08, 04/12, 05/03, 05/08, 05/12, 06/04, 06/08, 07/04, 07/08, 09/02
XPAYGRP2R	Pay Grade (E-1–E-4, E-5–E-9, W-1–W-5, O-1-O-3, O-4–O-6)	02/07, 03/03, 03/07, 04/04, 04/08, 04/12, 05/03, 05/08, 05/12, 06/04, 06/08, 06/12, 07/04, 07/04, 0708, 07/12, 08/01, 08/02, 08/03, 09/01, 09/02, 09/12, 10/06, 11/01
Educ	Educational attainment (high school or less, some college, college degree)	02/07, 03/03, 03/07, 03/11, 04/04, 04/08, 04/12, 05/03, 05/08, 05/12, 06/04, 06/08, 06/12, 07/04, 07/08, 07/12
Dependents	Has dependents (yes, no)	03/03, 03/07, 03/11, 04/04, 04/08, 04/12, 05/03, 05/08, 05/12, 06/04, 06/08, 06/12, 07/04, 07/04, 07/08, 07/12, 08/01, 08/02, 08/03, 09/01, 09/02, 09/12, 10/06, 11/01
College		
COLCREDR	College credits earned since joining: ANY	04/04, 06/04, 10/06, 12/06
Educational Opportunities		
Retention		
REASJNF	Great Influence: How much did each of the following contribute to your decision to join? Money for college, college repayment, education	07/12, 08/02,11/01,12/02,13/01
RETSEPI	Large Extent: To what extent is each of the following a reason for your leaving the service within the next 2 years? Continue my education	06/08, 08/02, 11/01, 12/02, 13/01
PRED1	Spouse completed Bachelor's or higher	03/07, 04/04, 06/04, 08/01, 10/06, 12/06

coded all Likert scale variables into binary format; responses of 4 or 5 were coded as agreement (satisfaction, likely, etc.), while responses of 1, 2, and 3 were coded as disagreement/lack of agreement. While we recognize that this decision means we will not utilize some of the available information, it strengthens our analyses by making the samples within each category larger. While "agreement" and "disagreement" are likely to be understood in a similar manner across individuals, it is less clear that individuals interpret "greatly decrease" and "somewhat decrease" consistently. Finally, collapsing

. (not at all to great influence); opportunities in the military versus civilian life (much better as civilian to much better in military).

the data in this manner means that we can run models of binary outcomes rather than models of multinomial outcomes; the interpretation of binary models is straightforward compared with that of multinomial models.

Next, we present a series of figures (E.1 through E.5) for each question included in our analyses in Chapter Six. For each question, we also calculate the probabilities that the stratified samples differ from each other, the probability that the answers change over time (for all groups), and the probability that the answers change over time for a single group. In the last case, this would suggest that the answers of one group changed, while the answers of others remained roughly constant.

Figure E.1
How Much Did Money for College, College Repayment, Contribute to Your Decision to Join?—Great Influence: by Pay Grade, Dependents, Years of Service, Education

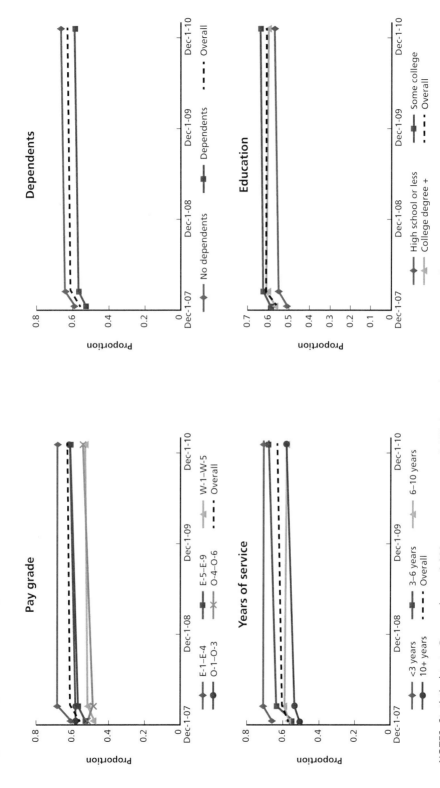

NOTES: *Statistical tests:* Pay grade: $p = 0.000$; survey wave: $p = 0.000$; interaction: $p = 0.768$. Years of service: $p = 0.000$; survey wave: $p = 0.023$; interaction: $p = 0.002$. Dependents: $p = 0.000$; survey wave: $p = 0.000$; interaction: $p = 0.011$. Education: $p = 0.000$; survey wave: $p = 0.064$; interaction: $p = 0.724$.

RAND *RR1766-E.1*

Figure E.2
College Credits Earned Since Joining—Any: by Pay Grade, Dependents, Years of Service, Education

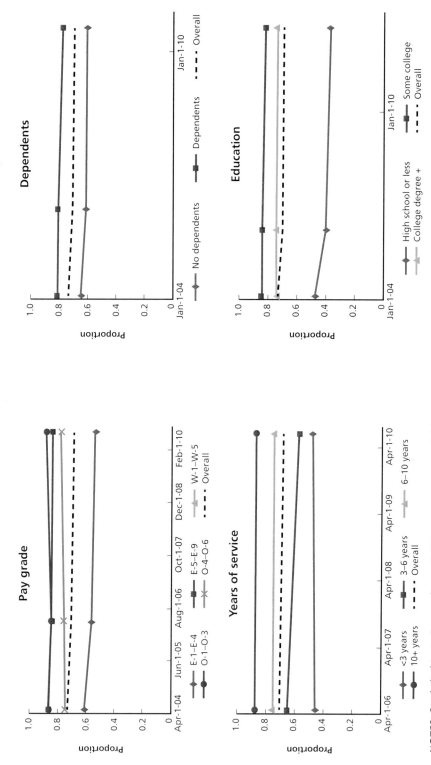

NOTES: *Statistical tests:* Pay grade: $p = 0.000$; survey wave: $p = 0.000$. Dependents: $p = 0.001$; interaction: $p = 0.000$. Dependents: $p = 0.001$; interaction: $p = 0.200$. Years of service: $p = 0.000$; survey wave: $p = 0.000$; interaction: $p = 0.448$; interaction: $p = 0.010$. Education: $p = 0.000$; survey wave: $p = 0.000$; interaction: $p = 0.009$.
RAND RR1766-E.2

Figure E.3
If Left Active Duty, Primary Activity Would Be College or University: by Pay Grade, Dependents, Years of Service, Education

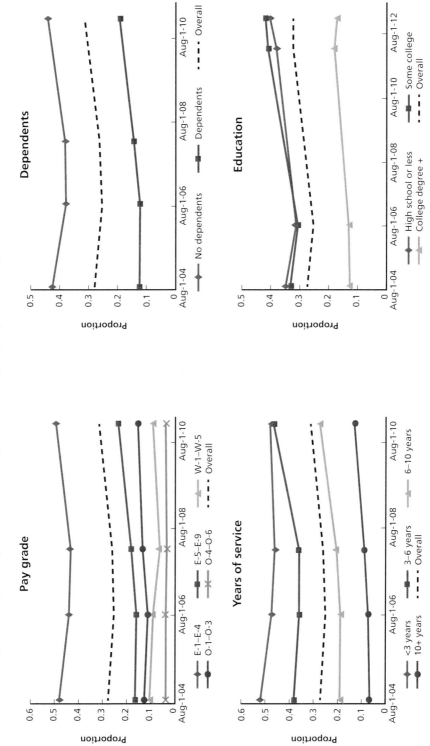

NOTES: *Statistical tests:* Pay grade: $p = 0.000$; survey wave: $p = 0.003$; interaction: $p = 0.000$. Dependents: $p = 0.000$; survey wave: $p = 0.000$; interaction: $p = 0.002$. Years of service: $p = 0.000$; survey wave: $p = 0.073$; interaction: $p = 0.000$. Education: $p = 0.000$; survey wave: $p = 0.006$; interaction: $p = 0.563$.
RAND RR1766-E.3

Figure E.4
To What Extent Is Continuing Your Education a Reason for Your Leaving the Service Within the Next 2 Years? - Large Extent: by Pay Grade, Dependents, Years of Service, Education

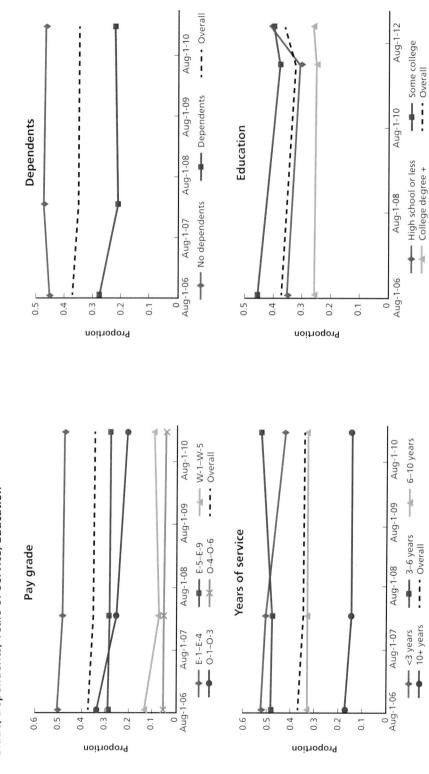

NOTES: *Statistical tests:* Pay grade: $p = 0.000$; survey wave: $p = 0.000$; interaction: $p = 0.670$; interaction: $p = 0.399$. Dependents: $p = 0.000$; survey wave: $p = 0.562$; interaction: $p = 0.399$. Dependents: $p = 0.000$; survey wave: $p = 0.201$; interaction: $p = 0.189$; interaction: $p = 0.240$. $p = 0.005$. Years of service: $p = 0.000$; survey wave: $p = 0.000$; interaction: $p = 0.383$. Education: $p = 0.000$; survey wave: $p = 0.000$; interaction: $p = 0.383$.

RAND RR1766-E.4

Figure E.5
Spouse Completed Bachelor's Degree or Higher: by Pay Grade, Dependents, Years of Service, Education

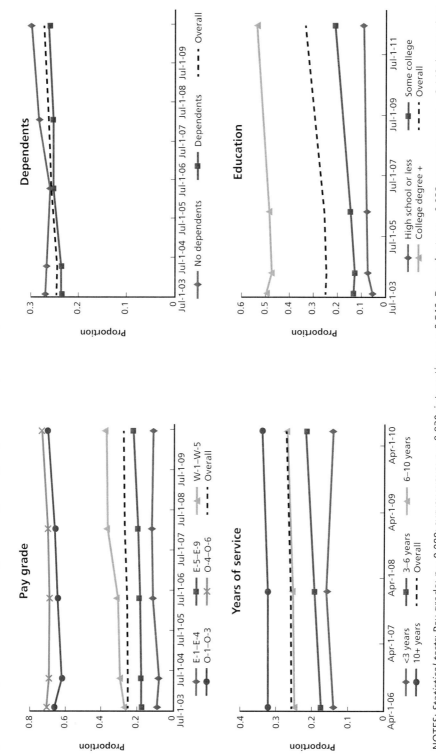

NOTES: *Statistical tests:* Pay grade: *p* = 0.000; survey wave: *p* = 0.000; interaction: *p* = 0.575. Years of service: *p* = 0.000; survey wave: *p* = 0.735; interaction: *p* = 0.030; interaction: *p* = 0.149; interaction: *p* = 0.000; survey wave: *p* = 0.131; interaction: *p* = 0.007.

RAND *RR1766-E.5*

References

American Council on Education, *Post 9/11 Veterans Educational Assistance Improvements Act of 2010*, memorandum, Hogan Lovells US LLP, Washington, D.C., 2011. As of April 4, 2017: https://www.hofstra.edu/pdf/sfs/financialaid/finaid_QA_%20Post911_veterans.pdf

Angrist, Joshua D., "Lifetime Earnings and the Vietnam Era Draft Lottery: Evidence from Social Security Administrative Records," *American Economic Review*, Vol. 80, No. 3, 1990, pp. 313–336.

Asch, Beth J., Paul Heaton, James Hosek, Francisco Martorell, Curtis Simon, and John T. Warner, *Cash Incentives and Military Enlistment, Attrition, and Reenlistment*, Santa Monica, Calif.: RAND Corporation, MG-950-OSD, 2010. As of April 4, 2017: http://www.rand.org/pubs/monographs/MG950.html

Asch, Beth J., M. Rebecca Kilburn, and Jacob A. Klerman, *Attracting College-Bound Youth into the Military: Toward the Development of New Recruiting Policy Options*, Santa Monica, Calif.: RAND Corporation, MR-984-OSD, 1999. As of April 4, 2017: http://www.rand.org/pubs/monograph_reports/MR984.html

Barr, Andrew, "Enlist or Enroll: The Effect of Changing Financial Aid Conditions on Military Enlistment," Charlottesville, Va.: University of Virginia, 2013.

———, "From the Battlefield to the Schoolyard: The Short-Term Impact of the Post-9/11 GI Bill," *Journal of Human Resources*, Vol. 50, No. 3, 2015, pp. 580–613.

Bound, John, and Sarah Turner, "Going to War and Going to College: Did World War II and the GI Bill Increase Educational Attainment for Returning Veterans?" *Journal of Labor Economics*, Vol. 20, No. 4, 2002, pp. 784–815.

Buddin, Richard J., *Success of First-Term Soldiers*, Santa Monica, Calif.: RAND Corporation, MG-262-A, 2005. As of April 4, 2017: http://www.rand.org/pubs/monographs/MG262.html

Buddin, Richard, and Kanika Kapur, "The Effect of Employer-Sponsored Education on Job Mobility: Evidence from the U.S. Navy," *Industrial Relations*, Vol. 44, No. 2, 2005, pp. 341–363.

Buryk, Peter, Thomas E. Trail, Gabriella C. Gonzalez, Laura L. Miller, and Esther M. Friedman, *Federal Educational Assistance Programs Available to Service Members: Program Features and Recommendations for Improved Delivery*, Santa Monica, Calif.: RAND Corporation, RR-664-OSD, 2015. As of April 4, 2017: http://www.rand.org/pubs/research_reports/RR664.html

Cataldi, E. F., C. Green, R. Henke, T. Lew, J. Woo, B. Shepherd, and P. Siegel, *2008–09 Baccalaureate and Beyond Longitudinal Study (B&B:08/09): First Look*, U.S. Department of Education, Washington, D.C.: National Center for Education Statistics, NCES 2011-236, July 2011. As of August 25, 2016:
https://nces.ed.gov/pubs2011/2011236.pdf

Card, David A., "The Causal Effect of Education on Earnings," in Orley C. Ashenfelter and David Card, eds., *Handbook of Labor Economics*, Vol. 3, Part A, Chapter 3, 1999, pp. 1801–1863.

CBO—*See* Congressional Budget Office.

Chromy, J. R., "Design Optimization with Multiple Objectives," in *Proceedings of the Section on Survey Research Methods*, Alexandria, Va.: American Statistical Association, 1987, pp. 194–199.

Congressional Budget Office, *Recruiting, Retention, and Future Levels of Military Personnel*, Washington, D.C., 2006.

Cordesman, Anthony H., and William Sullivan, *The Challenge of Meeting the Needs of Our Active and Reserve Military*, Washington, D.C.: Center for Strategic and International Studies, 2006. As of August 25, 2016:
https://www.csis.org/analysis/challenge-meeting-needs-our-active-and-reserve-military

Defense Manpower Data Center, "February 2012 Status of Forces Survey of Active Duty Members," in *Report No. 2012-037*, 2013.

Dimpfl, Thomas, and Stephan Jank, "Can Internet Search Queries Help to Predict Stock Market Volatility?" paper presented at December 2012 Finance Meeting EUROFIDAI-AFFI, Paris: European Financial Management, June 6, 2012.

DMDC—*See* Defense Manpower Data Center.

Eighmey, John, "Why Do Youth Enlist? Identification of Underlying Themes," *Armed Forces & Society*, No. 32, 2006.

Ettredge, Michael, John Gerdes, and Gilbert Karuga, "Using Web-Based Search Data to Predict Macroeconomic Statistics," *Communications of the ACM*, Vol. 48, No. 11, November 2005, pp. 87–92.

Farrell, Elizabeth F., "GI Blues," *Chronicle of Higher Education*, Vol. 51, No. 36, May 13, 2005, p. A31. As of August 25, 2016:
http://www.chronicle.com/article/GI-Blues/5396

Garcia, Federico, Jeremey Arkes, and Robert Trost, "Does Employer-Financed General Training Pay? Evidence from the US Navy," *Economics of Education Review*, Vol. 21, No. 1, 2002, pp. 19–27.

Gilpin, Gregory, and Michael S. Kofoed, "Employer-Sponsored Education Assistance and MBA Quality: An Application of the Alchian-Allen Substitution Hypothesis," SSRN working paper, December 1, 2015.

Ginsberg, Jeremy, Matthew H. Mohebbi, Rajan S. Patel, Lynnette Brammer, Mark S. Smolinski, and Larry Brilliant, "Detecting Influenza Epidemics Using Search Engine Query Data," *Nature*, Vol. 457, No. 7232, February 19, 2009, pp. 1012–1014.

Google AdWords, "Keyword Planner," online tool, undated. As of January 3, 2016:
http://adwords.google.com/KeywordPlanner

Jaeger, David A., and Marianne E. Page, "Degrees Matter: New Evidence on Sheepskin Effects in the Returns to Education," *Review of Economics and Statistics*, Vol. 78, No. 4, 1996, pp. 733–740.

Jahedi, Salar, Jennie W. Wenger, and Douglas Yeung, *78: Using Big Data to Identify the Concerns of Potential Recruits*, Santa Monica, Calif.: RAND Corporation, RR-1197-A, 2016. As of April 4, 2017: http://www.rand.org/pubs/research_reports/RR1197.html

Jepsen, Christopher, Kenneth Troske, and Paul Coomes, "The Labor-Market Returns to Community College Degrees, Diplomas, and Certificates," Journal of Labor Economics, Vol. 32, No. 1, 2014, pp. 95–121.

Kane, Thomas J., and Cecilia Elena Rouse, "Labor-Market Returns to Two- and Four-Year College," *American Economic Review*, Vol. 85, No. 3, 1995, pp. 600–614.

Loughran, David S., Paco Martorell, Trey Miller, and Jacob Alex Klerman, *The Effect of Military Enlistment on Earnings and Education*, Santa Monica, Calif.: RAND Corporation, TR-995-A, 2011. As of April 4, 2017: http://www.rand.org/pubs/technical_reports/TR995.html

Martorell, Paco, and Peter Bergman, *Understanding the Cost and Quality of Military-Related Education Benefit Programs*, Santa Monica, Calif.: RAND Corporation, RR-297-OSD, 2013. As of April 5, 2017: http://www.rand.org/pubs/research_reports/RR297.html

Page, Marianne E., "Fathers' Education and Children's Human Capital: Evidence from the World War II G.I. Bill," working paper, University of California-Davis, Department of Economics, undated.

Polich, J. Michael, Richard L. Fernandez, and Bruce R. Orvis, *Enlistment Effects of Military Educational Benefits*, Santa Monica, Calif.: RAND Corporation, N-1783-MRAL, 1982. As of April 4, 2017: http://www.rand.org/pubs/notes/N1783.html

Public Law 78-346, Serviceman's Readjustment Act, June 22, 1944.

Rostker, Bernard D., Jacob A. Klerman, Megan Zander-Cotugno, *Recruiting Older Youths: Insights from a New Survey of Army Recruits,* Santa Monica, Calif.: RAND Corporation, RR-247-OSD, 2014. As of April 4, 2017: http://www.rand.org/pubs/research_reports/RR247.html

Schmitz, Edward J., and Michael J. Moskowitz, "Analysis of the Post-9/11 GI Bill Benefits," Center for Naval Analyses, CRM D0020603.A2, 2009.

Search Engine Watch, "Yahoo Achieves Its Highest Search Share Since 2009," January 7, 2015. As of April 3, 2017: https://searchenginewatch.com/sew/news/2389193/yahoo-achieves-its-highest-search-share-since-2009

Segal, David R., Jerald G. Bachman, Peter Freedman-Doan, and Patrick M. O'Malley, "Propensity to Serve in the U.S. Military: Temporal Trends and Subgroup Differences," *Armed Forces & Society*, No. 25, 1999.

Shakely, Jack, "Dollar Signs in Uniform," *Los Angeles Times,* November 12, 2012. As of February 1, 2013: http://articles.latimes.com/2012/nov/12/opinion/la-oe-shakely-veterans-college-profit-20121112

Simon, Curtis J., Sebastian Negrusa, and John T. Warner, "Educational Benefits and Military Service: An Analysis of Enlistment, Reenlistment, and Veterans' Benefit Usage 1991–2005, *Economic Inquiry*, Vol. 48, No. 4, October 2010, pp. 1008–1031. As of February 1, 2013: http://onlinelibrary.wiley.com/doi/10.1111/j.1465-7295.2009.00233.x/full

Stanley, Marcus, "College Education and the Midcentury GI Bills," *Quarterly Journal of Economics*, Vol. 118, No. 2, 2003, pp. 671–708.

Steele, Jennifer L., Nicholas Salcedo, and James Coley, *Service Members in School: Military Veterans' Experiences Using the Post-9/11 GI Bill and Pursuing Post-Secondary Education*, Santa Monica, Calif.: RAND Corporation, MG-1083-ACE, 2011. As of April 4, 2017:
http://www.rand.org/pubs/monographs/MG1083.html

U.S. Department of Veterans Affairs, "GI Bill Comparison Tool," online tool, undated. As of May 11, 2017:
https://www.vets.gov/gi-bill-comparison-tool

———, *Pamphlet on the Montgomery GI Bill—Active Duty*, Pamphlet 22-90-2, Washington, D.C., 2011.

———, "Education and Training: Transfer Post-9/11 GI Bill to Spouse and Dependents," web page, updated December 5, 2013. As of May 28, 2014:
http://www.benefits.va.gov/gibill/post911_transfer.asp

———, "Education and Training: Post-9/11 GI Bill," web page, updated March 18, 2014. As of May 28, 2014:
http://www.benefits.va.gov/gibill/post911_gibill.asp

———, "National Center for Veterans Analysis and Statistics: Veteran Population, Fiscal Year 2016," updated April 15, 2016a. As of October 3, 2016:
https://www.va.gov/vetdata/veteran_population.asp

———, "Education and Training: Yellow Ribbon Program," updated June 29, 2016b. As of October 3, 2016:
http://www.benefits.va.gov/gibill/yellow_ribbon.asp

VA—*See* U.S. Department of Veterans Affairs.

Williamson, Vanessa, *A New GI Bill: Rewarding our Troops, Rebuilding our Military*, New York: Iraq and Afghanistan Veterans of America, 2008. As of April 4, 2017:
http://www.issuelab.org/resource/a_new_gi_bill_rewarding_our_troops_rebuilding_our_military